1-18-25

For there is nothing hidden that will not be disclosed,
and nothing concealed that will not be known
or brought out into the open.

—Luke 8:17 (NIV)

MYSTERIES OF COBBLE HILL FARM

Digging Up Secrets
Hide and Seek
Into Thin Air
Three Dog Knight
Show Stopper
A Little Bird Told Me
The Christmas Camel Caper
On the Right Track
Wolves in Sheep's Clothing
Snake in the Grass

MYSTERIES OF COBBLE HILL FARM

Snake in the Grass

ELIZABETH PENNEY

A Gift from Guideposts

Thank you for your purchase! We want to express our gratitude for your support with a special gift just for you.

Dive into *Spirit Lifters*, a complimentary e-book that will fortify your faith, offering solace during challenging moments. Its 31 carefully selected scripture verses will soothe and uplift your soul.

Please use the QR code or go to **guideposts.org/spiritlifters** to download.

Mysteries of Cobble Hill Farm is a trademark of Guideposts.

Published by Guideposts
100 Reserve Road, Suite E200, Danbury, CT 06810
Guideposts.org

Copyright © 2024 by Guideposts. All rights reserved. This book, or parts thereof, may not be reproduced, stored in a retrieval system, or transmitted in any form or by any means, electronic, mechanical, photocopying, recording, or otherwise, without the written permission of the publisher.

This is a work of fiction. While the setting of Mysteries of Cobble Hill Farm as presented in this series is fictional, the location of Yorkshire, England, actually exists, and some places and characters may be based on actual places and people whose identities have been used with permission or fictionalized to protect their privacy. Apart from the actual people, events, and locales that figure into the fiction narrative, all other names, characters, businesses, and events are the creation of the author's imagination and any resemblance to actual persons or events is coincidental. Every attempt has been made to credit the sources of copyrighted material used in this book. If any such acknowledgment has been inadvertently omitted or miscredited, receipt of such information would be appreciated.

Scripture references are from the following sources: *The Holy Bible, King James Version* (KJV). *The Holy Bible, New International Version* (NIV). Copyright © 1973, 1978, 1984, 2011 by Biblica, Inc. Used by permission of Zondervan. All rights reserved worldwide. www.zondervan.com.

Cover and interior design by Müllerhaus
Cover illustration by Bob Kayganich at Illustration Online LLC.
Typeset by Aptara, Inc.

ISBN 978-1-961441-24-8 (hardcover)
ISBN 978-1-961441-25-5 (softcover)
ISBN 978-1-961441-26-2 (epub)

Printed and bound in the United States of America
10 9 8 7 6 5 4 3 2 1

MYSTERIES OF COBBLE HILL FARM

Snake in the Grass

GLOSSARY OF UK TERMS

bobby • police officer

crisps • potato chips

crofter • one who rents and works a small farm

cuppa • a cup of tea

biscuit • cookie

boot • trunk of a vehicle

jumper • sweater, usually a pullover

ramble • a walk or hike

peckish • hungry

toad-in-the-hole • sausages in Yorkshire pudding batter

toff • a person who is often notably stylish or fashionable

wellies • Wellington boots

CHAPTER ONE

Spring had finally come to Cobble Hill Farm, in White Church Bay, Yorkshire. Yellow daffodils nodded in cheerful bunches, lambs gamboled in the fields, and the sun's warmth made a welcome return. New life unfurled in every direction, and as a result, Dr. Harriet Bailey had a bad case of spring fever.

Not that she wasn't busy. The vet practice had been slammed all day, on top of a busy week. "Goodbye," Harriet called to the last client, a woman with two cockapoos needing annual checkups. "Thanks for coming in." As soon as the door closed behind them, she faced Polly Thatcher, her twenty-five-year-old assistant. "Ready for a break? I'm wiped."

Polly tapped a few more keys then pushed back from her desk, ponytail swinging. "I sure am. Let's have tea and a snack, and then I'll finish the files."

Noticing the circles under her assistant's eyes, Harriet made an executive decision. "No you won't. It's Friday afternoon, and you're going home to put your feet up." Anticipating Polly's protest, she lifted a hand. "For once, Saturday appointments are sparse, so the paperwork can wait until Monday." The weather was supposed to be good this weekend, the first really warm March days, and people had plans.

Polly grinned as she rolled her chair forward. "I'll log out before you change your mind."

"And I'll go put the kettle on."

She went through the door into the main house. Last year, at age thirty-three, Harriet had moved from Connecticut to England to take over the veterinary practice owned by her late grandfather, Harold Bailey, and his father before him. She'd had big shoes to fill, and there had been some challenges, but Harriet now felt firmly established and at home in White Church Bay.

Harriet's lone regret was that she hadn't come to England sooner and worked with her grandfather before he died. According to her aunt, Dr. Jinny Garrett—a physician who lived in the dower cottage on the property—he had been very proud of Harriet and her achievements in the field. Harriet had been busy working in a large practice Stateside and planning to marry a fellow veterinarian.

Then that relationship had fallen apart, and her beloved grandfather had passed away, leaving his home and his practice to her. Her whole world had been turned upside down.

"Things have a way of working out for the best," Harriet murmured as she filled the kettle. She was dating Pastor Will Knight, a kind man and a good friend, on a casual basis. It was too soon to think about the future. She was having too much fun enjoying the present.

Wondering if she should have coffee instead, Harriet eyed the single-serve coffee machine, one of the few modern touches in the kitchen. The two-hundred-year-old stone farmhouse had never been fully renovated. Harriet appreciated the flagstone and wood floors, the plaster walls, and the beamed ceilings. It wasn't just a house, it was a piece of history—North Yorkshire's and her own.

She chose a French roast pod and started the coffeemaker. According to the temperature on the window thermometer, it was hovering in the fifties. Harriet decided they should sit outside in the sun for the first time since December, even though Yorkshire winters weren't quite as cold as Connecticut's. She hadn't missed the heaps of snow one bit. Her parents were a different story. She missed them every day. Hopefully, they would visit again soon, as they had for Thanksgiving.

Charlie, the clinic's calico cat, bolted into the room. The clinic's dachshund, Maxwell, was right behind her, the wheels that supported his paralyzed hindquarters spinning madly. Harriet laughed. "You two must have spring fever too." Their response was to hurry to her feet, where they looked up at her with hopeful eyes. "I'll give you snacks outside. How's that?"

The pets dashed to the french doors to wait, drawing another laugh from Harriet.

"What's going on?" Polly asked as she came through from the clinic.

"These guys." In the middle of preparing a tray, Harriet pointed with her chin. "I thought we could sit outside." Along with the pet treats, she added the latest goodies from her neighbor Doreen Danby, a great baker. "Doreen brought over raspberry-filled sugar cookies today."

"Oh, yum." Polly peered into the tin. "Love those." The kettle whistled, and she added a tea bag to a mug then filled it with boiling water.

Polly held the door for Harriet, who carried the tray, and the foursome paraded onto the back patio. Harriet narrowly avoided tripping over the eager dog and cat.

Harriet dispensed the pet treats before joining Polly at the table. The low afternoon sun still gave off heat, and she lifted her face to savor it. Her heart expanded with each breath of air tinged with the scent of green, growing things.

Then an all-too-familiar feeling of restlessness churned, and she squirmed in the chair, trying to get comfortable.

"What's up?" Polly asked. She didn't miss a trick—or any nuance indicating Harriet's state of mind. "You're frowning."

"I am?" Harriet rubbed her fingers across her forehead, hoping she wasn't developing lines. "I feel like a racehorse waiting for the gun to fire. I'm champing at the bit."

Polly nodded. "It's time for some new adventures. Winter can be a long, hard slog, one foot in front of the other, just trying to get through."

"You're absolutely right. Not to mention the dubious fun of dealing with snow and ice and bitter cold on farm visits." Harriet rolled her eyes. While many appointments had thankfully involved seeing animals in warm barns and shelters, she'd been out in the fields quite often.

She returned to Polly's first point. "When you said new adventures, did you have anything in mind?"

Polly leaned across the table, eagerness shining on her pretty face. "You know Captain Ezra?"

"He has a Newfoundland named Ursula. Yes." Harriet often remembered clinic clients by their pets.

"That's right. As you know, Captain Ezra does boat tours in the summer out of Whitby Harbor. He offered to take us out on Sunday if we wanted. He likes to perform a few trial runs to make sure everything is working right before the season starts."

"Us?" Harriet inquired. "Who else is going?"

Polly shrugged. "I'm not sure. 'Bring a friend—or two,' he said. That's why I asked you."

But not Detective Constable Van Worthington. Polly and Van had started dating last fall, only to have a rather dramatic breakup when Van proposed before Polly was ready. Harriet had seen indications that Polly was revisiting her decision, but the two were still wary around each other.

Harriet pulled out her phone. "I'll see if Will wants to go." As she typed the text, she asked, "Any other ideas?"

"Maybe." Polly snagged another cookie. "I'll give it some thought." After swallowing a bite, she said, "There should be some professional seminars, conferences, and workshops coming up too. Doc Bailey used to attend them now and again. He said they kept him sharp."

"That's a good point." Harriet thought back over the previous year as she sent the text. "With the move and settling in, I haven't been to anything like that here."

A car door slammed in the parking lot. "I wonder who that is," Polly said. "Your aunt's office is closed, right?" Like Harriet, Aunt Jinny's practice was attached to her home.

"I believe so. Maybe it's a visitor." Hopefully it wasn't an emergency for either of them, although people generally called first.

Two high, piping voices rang out, and a moment later, a boy and girl appeared around the corner, dressed in matching wool jumpers, as sweaters were called here, and jeans. "Harriet!" they cried. Sophie and Sebastian Garrett were Aunt Jinny's twin grandchildren.

The pair engulfed Harriet in hugs. "What are you doing here?" she asked.

"We came for the weekend," Sebastian said. "We all got out early today."

"Do your parents know you're over here?" Harriet asked. "And say hello to Polly."

"Hello, Polly," they chorused obediently.

"We told them we were going to play out here," Sophie added to Harriet.

Next door, Aunt Jinny emerged from her house and waved, letting Harriet know she was aware of the twins' location. "Stay right here." She watched Aunt Jinny settle at her backyard table, obviously planning to keep an eye on them.

"We will," the twins promised. Then they noticed the tin of cookies. "Can we have one?" Sebastian asked.

In response, Harriet held up the tin so Aunt Jinny could see it and then pointed at the youngsters. Aunt Jinny put up one finger.

"Just one," Harriet said. The pair took their time studying the choices, then each took a cookie and ran off.

"They are so cute," Polly said.

Harriet's phone beeped. "Will would like to go. What time should I tell him?" As the local minister, he was tied up with church duties all morning on Sundays.

"One o'clock in Whitby," Polly said. "We can bring a picnic lunch on the boat."

Whitby wasn't too far. "So come back here after church and change, grab our lunch, and go?" Harriet mused. "It's a plan."

The twins were poking around the stone wall, followed closely by Charlie and Maxwell. Harriet smiled, thinking about the days she'd been content to play outside with nothing but her imagination.

Next door, Aunt Jinny's son, Anthony, and his wife, Olivia, emerged from the house, tea mugs in hand. As they settled at the table, Harriet said, "Let's go say hi." She grabbed her mug and the tin of cookies.

Polly readily followed, having already formed friendships with the couple, who were about Harriet's age. The family lived in nearby Pickering, and Anthony was a pharmacist while Olivia worked as a kindergarten teacher.

Olivia jumped up as the women approached, and hugged them. "So good to see you. We're here for a relaxing evening." She winked. "I hope."

Anthony had risen to his feet to hug his cousin. "We've both been going at a breakneck pace lately. As for the children, they have a bad case of spring fever."

Sebastian was attempting to shimmy up a large tree trunk while Sophie walked on top of the low wall. "Be careful," their mother called. The twins waved but kept on.

"We all do," Harriet said, pulling out a chair. "Cookie—I mean, biscuit?" She offered the tin.

"Don't mind if I do," Anthony said, selecting one. "We're getting fish and chips tonight, and nothing dampens my appetite for that meal."

Olivia laughed. "That one has a hollow leg."

"Tell me about it," Aunt Jinny said. "Couldn't keep him full when he was a boy."

"That sounds good," Harriet said. "Would you mind if I join you?" Cliffside Chippy, a short walk down the public path to the village, was one of Harriet's favorite eateries.

Polly lifted a hand. "Me too, if that's okay. I don't have any dinner plans."

Aunt Jinny regarded her with a sympathetic gaze. She knew all about Polly and Van. "You're both welcome. Anytime."

The twins were now kneeling on the ground, studying the stone wall. Sebastian lowered himself even farther, almost lying down, and reached his hand into what looked like a cavity.

Harriet stood up to see better, hoping they hadn't come across a bee's nest or an animal that might bite them.

Sebastian scrambled to his feet, something clutched in both hands, and ran toward the adults, Sophie on his heels.

"Look what I found," he said when he arrived at the table.

Olivia pulled away with a shriek. "That lizard is huge!"

Harriet's heart rate spiked. This was no native reptile. Dull gray, with patches of rusty orange and a small dorsal crest, it looked like an iguana, albeit a species she'd never seen before. Someone's stray pet? With lows still in the thirties, it wasn't safe for this tropical animal to remain loose.

Harriet held out her hands. "Give it to me."

Sebastian readily handed over the creature, whose round dark eyes barely blinked. Its body was a little over a foot long, and it weighed under a pound, if she had to guess.

"Any idea what kind it is?" Anthony asked. "I've never seen one like that before."

"Not off the top of my head." Harriet looked at Polly. "Want to take a picture and do an image search?" While not infallible, an online search would be a start. "We can also post the picture on the local bulletin boards in case someone lost him. Or her." Harriet hadn't treated iguanas or many reptiles before, so she would appreciate help with identification.

Harriet held the iguana in both hands so Polly could get a full-length picture. Fortunately, the lizard didn't pull out of her grip and run. Instead, it seemed quite content to rest.

Everyone waited as Polly searched on her phone. After a couple of minutes, she gasped. "You're not going to believe this." She turned the screen to show them. "It's an endangered rock iguana from the Caribbean. There are only a couple hundred of them left in the world."

CHAPTER TWO

Harriet regarded the new arrival with even greater interest. "How did you get here?" she asked. To Polly, she said, "Can you look up how to tell whether it's male or female?"

Still holding the reptile on her lap, Harriet sipped coffee, pondering what her next course of action should be. What did one do after finding an endangered species in the UK? This situation was definitely outside her experience. In the States, there would be agencies to contact, protocols to follow. It must be the same here, except she hadn't dealt with the correct authorities yet.

The twins flanked Harriet, one on each side. "Can we name it?" Sophie asked.

"Once we figure out if it's a boy or a girl," Harriet said.

"Got it. Change seats with me, Jinny?" Once settled, Polly showed Harriet a diagram.

Harriet gently turned the iguana over to compare it with the pictures. "This one is a girl."

The twins, eyes still on the iguana, whispered and debated. Finally, Sophie stepped forward. "Her name is Mango."

"That's perfect," Harriet said, impressed. Mangoes grew in the Caribbean, among other places. Did the twins know that? "Why did you pick Mango?"

Sebastian shrugged. "'Cause she's got some orange on her. And I like mangoes."

Mango squirmed, and Harriet realized she'd better cage the animal before it escaped. "I'm going to take Mango inside and call an exotic animal vet. There's a clinic in York."

"Good idea," Aunt Jinny said. "You don't want to lose the poor thing."

"Can we come with you?" Sebastian asked.

Harriet stood, holding the lizard firmly with both hands. "Of course. Polly, can you get the door for me?" The clinic was locked.

Thankfully, Harriet managed to hang on to Mango and get her safely into a small cage in the rear of the clinic. "She's probably thirsty. Sebastian, can you fill this water dish?" Harriet handed him a small one made to hang inside the cage.

"What does Mango eat?" Sophie asked, concern in her voice. "She's probably hungry."

"Dr. Jason Peel is head of the clinic," Polly called from the reception desk. "Should I try his direct line?"

"Please." To Sophie, she said, "I'm not sure about Mango's diet. We'll find out in a few minutes, okay? Then we'll get her a meal."

Sebastian had filled the water dish, and Harriet helped him secure it inside the cage. Then she made sure the door was firmly latched.

"He's on line one," Polly said as she joined them. "You two want to do some coloring while Harriet is on the phone?" She led the way back to the waiting room, where they kept coloring books featuring animals for young visitors.

Harriet picked up the closest phone. "Dr. Peel? This is Dr. Harriet Bailey. I'm a vet at the Cobble Hill clinic in White Church Bay. I need your advice."

"Certainly. Please, call me Jason." His voice was friendly and warm, which released the tension in Harriet's shoulders. He sounded like he wanted to help. "What can I do for you, Dr. Bailey?"

"Call me Harriet." She paced, watching the iguana licking at the water. "I have a situation here. Some young children found a rare iguana hiding in a stone wall in my back garden."

"Rare?" he repeated. "How rare?"

"Very, if I'm right. It matches the photos online of a San Salvador rock iguana." Harriet picked up her cell phone to view the information Polly had forwarded. "*Cyclura rileyi.*"

Jason was silent for a long moment. "Those are among the rarest iguanas on earth."

"So I've been told." Harriet shrugged helplessly. "I have no idea where Mango—"

"Mango?"

"The kids named her. Listen, I'll send you some pictures. If you think I'm right, can you tell me what to do? I have to report this somewhere, right?"

"Local police, then Border Force. Perhaps the Wildlife Crimes Unit. But we're getting ahead of ourselves here. Maybe it's not a rare iguana and someone's pet escaped."

Harriet let out a breath. "I would prefer that scenario. If you'll give me a cell number or an email, I'll send pictures ASAP. Oh, and what should I give her to eat?"

"Iguanas are herbivores. She can have vegetables and a little fruit." He reeled off a list.

To her relief, Harriet had several items on hand. "I have romaine lettuce, green beans, and mushrooms."

"Good. I'll text you back the full list when you send the photos," Jason said. He gave her a number, which she wrote down.

"I'll do it right now. Will you call me with any information you receive?"

"You bet."

Harriet hung up the clinic phone and grabbed her cell to take the photos. She moved close to the cage, wondering what to do about the metal grid. The iguana was in the far corner, watching her warily, so she hastily opened the door and took several shots. Then she withdrew her hand and shut the door again.

She was scrolling through the shots when Polly returned. "What did he say?" she asked.

"Not much." Harriet selected the two clearest images, attached them to a short text message, then sent it to Jason.

Less than a minute later, her phone rang. Harriet read the screen and answered. "Hey, Jason. What do you think?"

He seemed to have trouble articulating. "Harriet," he finally choked out, "your identification is correct. That is a San Salvador rock iguana. Exporting them is forbidden, so this is a criminal matter."

Harriet's stomach clenched. "What do we do?"

"Stand by. I'm calling the authorities and will be back in touch. Probably nothing will happen until tomorrow. Meanwhile, give the iguana food and water. Don't, under *any* circumstances, let her out of that cage."

Early the next morning, Harriet unlocked the clinic door, her heart beating much faster than normal. How many times had she checked on the iguana since yesterday afternoon? At least half a dozen.

Each time, she had been afraid that she would find it gone, ill, or worse. How long had Mango been loose in the English countryside? Surely the spring temperatures weren't nearly warm enough for a tropical reptile. She'd cranked up the heat last night to make sure the iguana would be comfortable.

Mango ate heartily when the twins gave her vegetables, Harriet reminded herself as she switched on the lights. Still, she held her breath as she hurried to the back to check the cage.

The iguana was still in her corner, and when she saw Harriet, she trundled forward as if to say hello.

"Good morning to you too," Harriet said, laughing with relief. She checked the water dish, which was almost empty. "I'll get you some more water, and breakfast." Iguanas liked bananas with skin on, according to Jason, and she happened to have one.

After filling the water, Harriet returned to the house. There she made coffee, prepared three meals, and fed Charlie, Maxwell, and Mango. Then she ate cold cereal and milk with the rest of the banana. Peeled.

Knocking on the back door startled her, and Harriet looked up to see two little faces pressed to the glass. The twins, freshly scrubbed and wearing corduroy pants and jumpers. "Well, hello," she said, letting them in. "I'm guessing you're here to see—"

"Mango," they finished for her in unison.

"Is she awake?" Sebastian asked, his expression serious. "I wouldn't want to disturb her. She's probably tired after traveling all that way."

Last night, over fish and chips at Cliffside Chippy, Harriet had explained where Mango was from, even showing the twins a map. She didn't mention the fact that this new resident was probably the victim of a crime, although she told the adults later, after the twins went to bed.

Will had joined the group, and they'd all enjoyed a lively board game with frequent breaks for Harriet to check Mango.

"She's awake," Harriet said. "I already gave her breakfast." She pulled four grapes off a bunch and gave them each two. "You can give her these."

"I like grapes too," Sophie said.

Harriet smiled. "You can have some after." She'd make sure they washed their hands first.

While the twins were feeding Mango, Harriet went to the front door and unlocked it. Jason would be there soon, along with an official from the Border Force. A local officer was also supposed to arrive, as the police were the first line of defense for wildlife crimes, according to Jason.

That would probably be Van, Polly's former boyfriend. In a situation like that, Harriet might expect fireworks. But with these two, it was covert glances and stoic smiles.

Harriet wished Polly and Van would make up. They were perfect together, and they clearly weren't over each other. They had managed a tentative friendship, but Harriet suspected that wouldn't be enough for either for long.

Van was first to arrive, his round, pleasant face beaming under his brimmed cap. "I understand you've got a very unusual visitor here."

"You can say that again." Harriet showed him to the cage, where the twins were still watching every move the iguana made.

The detective constable crouched beside the children. "Well, how about that? I've never seen an iguana that color. To be honest, I haven't seen many at all. Maybe the occasional green one owned by a friend."

"She's very rare," Sebastian said. "An endangered species."

Van threw him a surprised look. "Is that so?" He peered more closely. "What's that you're giving her to eat?"

Thrilled, Sophie and Sebastian began to share all they knew about Mango while Van listened attentively. He was great with children. Harriet wished she could freeze the scene in place so Polly could see it.

Someone rang the bell, and Harriet hastened to answer. Two men stood on the step. One was about Harriet's age, with curly brown hair and jeans that made her suspect he was her fellow vet. The older man wore a black uniform, his gray hair close-cropped under a cap.

"Dr. Peel," Harriet said, offering her hand to the younger man, "I'm Dr. Bailey." With the authorities there, she thought she should keep things on a formal footing.

"Nice to meet you, Dr. Bailey." Jason played along. "This is Officer Darren Crosby, Border Force out of Whitby."

"Pleased to meet you, Doc." Officer Crosby had cool, pale blue eyes. In contrast to Jason, his demeanor was reserved, almost stiff.

"The iguana is in the back," Harriet said. "Follow me."

Van and the children were still grouped around the cage. The detective constable noticed them first, straightening with a hand to his hat. "Hello. DC Worthington," he said to Jason. He nodded to the Border Force agent. "Officer Crosby."

Harriet wasn't surprised they knew each other in such a small, rural area where interagency cooperation was important.

Jason introduced himself and then moved to the cage. "Hello," he said to the twins. "I'm Dr. Peel. I'm going to take a look at your iguana, if that's all right."

"It's fine with us," Sebastian said. "Her name is Mango."

"I like that." Jason opened the cage and with a deft, gentle grip, extracted the iguana from the cage and examined her. "Female," he observed. "In surprisingly good health. I'd venture to say she hasn't been loose long."

"I suppose that's something to go on," Officer Crosby said. "I checked with Heathrow to see if they've caught any iguanas lately. Also to give them a heads-up that this one came through."

"Heathrow?" Harriet was surprised. "That's over two hundred miles from here."

Officer Crosby folded his arms. "A lot of exotic animals come in through the airlines. Some via cargo ships as well. We don't normally see much animal trade up here. Coming in, I mean. Poachers sometimes send them the other way, to mainland Europe and beyond."

"So a smuggler could have brought her from London?" Harriet asked. "And she somehow escaped?"

"A smuggler or someone who bought her," Jason said. "Keep an eye out for people advertising a lost iguana. They might think people won't know how rare and special she is." He put Mango back inside the cage and closed the door.

Van was taking notes. "I'll be sure to keep an eye online and monitor the local grapevine as well."

Officer Crosby had taken out his phone and was snapping pictures of Mango. "Animal smuggling is a big problem in the UK, as with anywhere else. We've found lion cubs in luggage. Rare birds tucked into tubes. Suitcases full of turtles."

"That's horrible." Such cruel treatment of precious animals made Harriet's heart ache. The poor things were carelessly ripped away from their natural environments with no thought for their welfare. Those who did it cared only about profit.

"It upsets me too," Jason said, his kind eyes studying her face. "That's why we all need to work together to stop smuggling."

"I'll do my best," Van said.

The door opened, and Polly entered. She faltered when she saw the group. "Oh, hello."

"Polly, this team is here to assist us with Mango," Harriet said. She made the introductions and then gave Polly a brief overview. "What do we do with her now?" she asked Officer Crosby. "Are you going to take her into custody?"

He shook his head. "There's a possibility, due to the rareness of this species, that she'll be sent home. We'll need to coordinate with the Bahamian authorities first. We don't have the facilities ourselves, so we usually house the animals in wildlife rescue centers or zoos."

"Speaking of which," Jason chimed in, "I have the perfect place for Mango. Moorland Zoo, located at Langford Hall, not far from here. I already took the liberty of speaking to Victoria Langford, and she's willing to take the iguana later today, if that works for you. She has a lot of expertise caring for reptiles."

"I've known Victoria since our school days," Polly said. "She's wonderful."

"We love going to Moorland Zoo," Sebastian piped up. "Can we go with you?"

"Please, Harriet?" Sophie's eyes were pleading.

"I don't see why not," Harriet said. She was relieved to learn there was a solution. While she didn't mind housing an extra animal or two, she was far from a reptile expert. Mango was too rare to be left in inexperienced hands. "We'll ask your parents. I'm not sure what plans they have today."

The twins cheered. "We'll go ask them," Sophie said. They bolted out of the room, chattering with excitement.

"Whew," Harriet said. "I thought they might be upset about Mango leaving."

Van closed his notebook. "I'm glad to know she'll be well cared for."

Sensing that the meeting was drawing to a close, Harriet said, "Would you all like a cup of tea before you head out? We have a few minutes before our first patient, don't we, Polly?"

"We sure do." Polly headed for the connecting door. "I'll put the kettle on."

Van watched Polly go. "Thanks for the offer, but I'd better be on my way. I'll be in touch, Dr. Bailey."

Jason and Officer Crosby stayed for tea, served by Polly, who seemed disappointed that Van had left. But perhaps that was wishful thinking on Harriet's part.

And a very informative meeting it was. Harriet felt she was getting a crash course in wildlife smuggling and the challenges that came with it. Jason said that a large portion of his vet work consisted of examining and caring for confiscated animals. The rest was consulting with zoos and private owners of exotic pets.

Officer Crosby excused himself first, explaining that he had a lot to do.

As Jason was leaving, he made a surprising proposal. "As you can imagine, as the lone exotic animal vet in the county, I'm stretched pretty thin most of the time. It'd be wonderful if I could call on you to fill in occasionally."

Fill in? As in take care of animals she'd never seen up close, let alone studied?

Biting her lip as she wondered how to respond, Harriet pictured a procession of lions, tigers, bears, and giraffes needing her services. Not to mention snakes. She shuddered.

She'd wanted a new challenge. *Be careful what you wish for, right?*

CHAPTER THREE

Apparently seeing the confusion on her face, Jason said, "I'm sorry. I can see I've overwhelmed you."

"I'm not exactly well-versed in exotic animals," Harriet managed to say.

"Understood," Jason said. "It's just that I'm supposed to go on vacation next week. Usually, a vet from Manchester covers for me, but she's out on maternity leave."

As a single-practitioner operation, Harriet understood his dilemma. "I'll give it a try during your vacation. How's that? Are there other vets I can call for backup?" There must be other exotic vets in the UK. She could consult them by phone and exchange photos and videos if needed, to assist in diagnosis and treatment. She'd done that with Jason. Plus, she'd called other vets in the area when she came across a perplexing case.

"Absolutely," Jason said. "I'll introduce you to my network before I leave."

Harriet checked the time. Her patient was due any minute. "I'll see you at the zoo later?"

"Definitely." He smiled. "You'll like Victoria. She's awesome."

With that, he waved goodbye and strode toward his vehicle.

Another car pulled into the parking lot, and Harriet recognized her client, the owner of a large sheepdog.

The spring breeze was warm and soft, so Harriet lingered outside until the pair reached her. "Good morning," she said, holding the clinic door open. "Isn't it a lovely day?"

After lunch, Harriet loaded Mango's cage into her Land Rover—or the Beast, as she affectionately called it—for the trip to Moorland Zoo. Accompanying her were Aunt Jinny and the twins, who were beside themselves with excitement. Olivia and Anthony planned to take a nice long walk along the cliffside path while they were gone.

Harriet typed the zoo's address into her GPS. "Should take us about twenty minutes to get there." The zoo was located on the fringe of the famous Yorkshire moors.

"You don't need that to navigate," Aunt Jinny said. "I know the way to Moorland Zoo. Went there many times with my dad."

"Did Grandad treat the animals there? I had no idea." Harriet put the Land Rover into gear, and they set off. She was careful to drive smoothly so as not to jostle the iguana.

"Sometimes," Aunt Jinny said. "He was good friends with Sir Percy Langford, who founded the zoo in the 1950s, and Victoria's father, Marshall Langford, who took over. Marshall died a few months ago."

"How sad. Does Victoria have siblings?"

"Only a brother, Nick. He passed away twenty years ago, along with his cousin, Scott Spencer. A boating accident."

Imagining the family's grief, Harriet felt a pang of sadness. "That's awful."

"It was." Aunt Jinny stared out the window, silent for a moment. Then she seemed to shake herself. "Anyway. You'll like the zoo. The Langfords have done a nice job there. And Victoria is a sweetheart."

Harriet made a mental note to go through Grandad's journals later. The fact he'd treated exotic animals was a revelation. Maybe she could learn more about this zoo and her grandfather's patients there. Since discovering the journals, Harriet had consulted them frequently for insight about the vet practice, the local area, and its residents.

Their route led them deep into the countryside. The North York Moors National Park encompassed over 100,000 acres of rolling hills of heather and gorse, rock formations, and bogs. Picturesque, often lonely, and true wilderness.

"I really want to get out on the trails this year," Harriet said. Maybe she should add regular hikes to her schedule. People came from all over the world to walk around the moors.

"Take a map, compass, and provisions with you if you do," Aunt Jinny said. "Ramblers get lost out there every year. Unfortunately, they try to depend on their cell phones for help. That doesn't always work, because service on the moors is spotty at best."

"Same thing happens in the States." Reminded of technology, she glanced at the navigation device, which had stopped responding. "Speaking of not working, it seems you'll have to take over directions after all."

With Aunt Jinny's guidance, they were soon approaching the zoo, which was announced by several signs.

Sebastian and Sophie bounced in their seats. "We're almost there, Nana," Sebastian exclaimed.

"Keep your eyes peeled for the elephant," Sophie cried. "That's what Daddy always says."

"The elephant?" Harriet inquired. "They have one of those?"

"They do," Aunt Jinny said. "That's not what Sophie means though."

Just as Harriet glimpsed a set of open gates, she saw the elephant. It was an enormous fiberglass sculpture standing guard over a sign with scrolling letters: MOORLAND ZOO. EST. 1955.

Then she noticed a small cluster of people blocking the entrance and waving signs. Slowing the Beast to a crawl, she asked, "What's this?"

"Protestors," Aunt Jinny said. "I heard they've been picketing zoos."

Now Harriet could read the signs. FREE THE ANIMALS. WILD ANIMALS SHOULD BE WILD. ZOOS ARE CRUEL. A red circle with zoo in the middle and a big line through it.

The lead protester appeared to be a woman about Harriet's age. Her red hair was bound in a long braid that swung as she shouted and waved her sign.

"What are they doing, Nana?" Sophie asked.

Talk about a difficult situation to explain to young ones. But Aunt Jinny seemed prepared for it. "Some people don't like zoos. And they have a right to their opinion as long as they don't harm anyone."

"I like zoos," Sebastian said stoutly. Then he added in a doubtful tone, "I think."

"We'll talk about it once we're inside," Aunt Jinny said in a comforting voice.

Harriet stopped near the protestors, who were blocking the drive. "Excuse me," she called. "I need to get through."

The redhead sauntered over with a flip of her braid. "Why's that? The zoo isn't open right now."

"So why are you here?" Harriet asked. Surely their protesting wasn't as effective without an audience.

The woman smiled and pointed. "Because of them."

A glance in the rearview mirror revealed a news van pulling up behind the Beast. "Please let me pass," Harriet repeated. "I'm a veterinarian, and I'm here for a patient." She showed the woman the vet association card from her wallet.

"Dr. Harriet Bailey," the woman muttered, reading the card. She handed it back to Harriet and yelled, "Stand aside, everyone. Medical personnel coming through."

The protesters edged out of the way, and Harriet eased past them. "Wow. I wasn't expecting that."

"Neither was I," Aunt Jinny said. "Though I've heard of it happening in other places."

Gravel crunched as they pulled into a large parking lot where, to Harriet's relief, Jason awaited them beside his car. The rest of the lot was empty, so the place did appear to be closed. Harriet vaguely recalled limited hours on the website she'd briefly perused.

Harriet swung into a spot beside Jason's vehicle. Aunt Jinny helped the children out of the car as Harriet approached him. "Quite the scene out there." She jerked a thumb toward the gates.

He shrugged. "I had to run the gauntlet as well. I hope they didn't give you too bad a time."

"Not after I said I was a vet. And guess what? A news crew just showed up."

Jason shook his head. "Glad neither of us got caught up in that. I don't like being put on the spot. Which has happened more than once."

"I'm sure." She imagined that, working with exotic animals, he frequently had to deal with questions concerning their origin and the best approach to caring for them.

She took a moment to orient herself. To her left was a gateway with a kiosk and signs denoting the entrance to the zoo. Beyond were trees so tall, she couldn't see any animals or their enclosures.

To her right was a hedge broken by a path and, a little farther along, a narrow lane. Beyond the hedge and several large trees was the house, a sprawl of chimneys and gables. She guessed the lane provided access to the house and grounds. Signs at both the path and the lane read, PRIVATE. NO ENTRANCE.

"Where are we taking Mango?" Harriet asked.

"To the house," Jason said. "Victoria has a facility in the old conservatory for certain animals."

"Lead on," she told him.

Jason took the cage from the Land Rover then led them through the hedge and along a winding path to the house. Straight ahead, a row of tall glass windows set in black ironwork glinted in the sun. The conservatory.

"This is a beautiful property," Aunt Jinny said. "It's been in the Langford family for generations."

"How did they happen to start a zoo?" Harriet asked.

"I'll let Victoria fill you in on that," Aunt Jinny said. "Children," she called out, "no running." Ahead of them, Sebastian and Sophie slowed obediently.

As they approached the conservatory, one of several french doors opened, and a young woman with short dark hair and a spray of freckles across her pert nose stepped out with a smile. "There you are. Right this way."

The children were the first to enter, followed by the adults. "Hello, Victoria," Aunt Jinny said. "This is my niece, Dr. Harriet Bailey."

Harriet smiled and said, "Please, call me Harriet."

"It's so nice to meet you, Harriet," Victoria said as they crossed the threshold. "I'm Victoria Langford. I've heard so much about you. Your grandfather was always a favorite around here. Jinny, it's lovely to see you again. It's been forever." Victoria smiled at the children. "Who are these intrepid animal wranglers?"

The twins giggled as Aunt Jinny made introductions. Meanwhile, Jason set the cage on the tiled floor, next to a large cage containing climbs, tree branches, and other features. Harriet noticed several other cages in the large room, which was kept at tropical-level temperatures and humidity. Mango would love her new home.

"Open that cage right there, please," Victoria told Jason, pointing. She bent to open the transport cage and gently gathered Mango with both hands. "Aren't you a beauty?" she murmured. "So far from home, poor thing. We'll get you all squared away, I promise."

"Her name is Mango," Sebastian said. "Sophie and I named her."

"Perfect choice," Victoria said with approval. After checking the iguana over, she said, "She appears to be in really good condition."

To the children, she said, "I understand you were in charge of her meals. Can you tell me what you fed her?"

They both began to talk at once. While listening, Victoria placed Mango in the empty cage, where she was soon scurrying around, exploring.

"That's quite an upgrade," Harriet said. "My clinic cages definitely weren't adequate." Not to mention that she couldn't let Mango out to run in the enclosed yard as she did with the dogs who boarded at the clinic.

"You probably don't get many stray reptiles," Victoria said with a smile. Her expression sobered. "And I hope there aren't any more out there."

"I never thought of that," Harriet said with dismay. "We'll have to search the property, just in case."

Jason watched as Mango began climbing up a branch. "If a shipment went astray, then yes, there could be more. I'll ask the police to send out a notice suggesting that people keep their eyes open." He turned to Harriet. "Do you mind being one of the contact points?"

"Not at all. If Mango got loose in White Church Bay…"

"Then there could be others close by," Victoria said.

"If we find more, I'll be calling you both," Harriet said. She was out of her depth here. The experts were needed when it came to endangered species.

"Please do, anytime," Victoria urged. "I understand you'll be filling in for Jason while he's away."

Surprised that she already knew, Harriet cut her eyes toward Jason, who shrugged. "I am, yes. Jason will connect me to other exotic animal vets, in case I need advice or help."

"Wonderful." Victoria smiled at the twins. "I have fresh lemonade if you'd like some. Or we can have tea. Then I thought I'd give you a tour."

"A tour?" The twins bounced with excitement.

"That is a treat," Aunt Jinny said. "Especially since you're currently closed to visitors. Are you sure you have time?"

"Absolutely," Victoria said. "As long as you do."

"I'd love a tour," Harriet confirmed.

The twins cheered and hugged her.

Victoria ushered Sebastian and Sophie toward another cage. "While I get our refreshments, I'd like you to do me a favor. See how many genets you can find."

"What's a genet?" Sebastian asked.

Aunt Jinny pulled a picture up on her phone, which she showed to the children. Genets were small, spotted mammals with pointed noses and long, ringed tails. "Genets are related to the cat family but more closely to mongooses."

Jason accompanied Victoria to the kitchen while the children counted genets. The twins were overjoyed when they spotted the pretty creatures nestled behind foliage or hiding among rocks.

"They're nocturnal," Harriet said, after reading up on them. "They like to sleep all day."

"Who wants biscuits?" Victoria called out as she returned to the conservatory. She held a tin while Jason carried a tray. He set it on a table in one corner, and they gathered for refreshments.

"We counted four genets," Sophie informed Victoria. "Is that all of them?"

"Yes, it is," Victoria replied. "Good job."

The twins beamed at her as they settled at the table.

As Harriet sipped tea and nibbled on a cookie, she observed Mango and the genets. This had to be one of the most unusual tea breaks she'd ever had. She was almost as excited as the children at the prospect of seeing the other unusual animals housed at the zoo.

God's creation was truly magnificent, so varied and fascinating. Harriet sighed with joy. Her plan to shake up her routine was off to a great start.

CHAPTER FOUR

"My grandfather, Sir Percy Langford, founded the zoo about sixty years ago," Victoria explained at the beginning of the tour. "This was back in the days when collecting wild animals wasn't fraught with controversy. In fact, the zoo was a continuation of a tradition first started by his grandfather. In those days, gentlemen of a certain class often enjoyed seeking out the unusual."

"A competitive sport in some cases," Aunt Jinny said. "Or so my father told me."

Victoria pressed a button to open the gate to the zoo itself. "And he was right. Harold Bailey was a great favorite around here. Both my grandfather and dad thought very highly of him."

"Our Dr. Harold Bailey?" Sebastian asked. "Our great-grandfather?"

"Exactly so, Sebastian," Victoria said. "Your great-grandfather often took care of the animals for us. And now we hope Dr. *Harriet* Bailey will do the same."

"I'd be delighted to," Harriet said. "Whenever I can."

Victoria went on with her introduction. "Our focus now is conservation, education, and working to protect and build endangered species. My late father, Marshall, was a pioneer in much of this work. Now I'm proud to carry it forward into the future."

"I wish those protestors could understand that," Aunt Jinny observed. "You're actually on the same side."

"We are." Victoria's smile was rueful. "I'd love to return all our animal friends to the wild. Unfortunately, it's not practical—or safe for them. Many were born in captivity or have been here long enough that they've grown used to having their needs provided for. They no longer have the ability to take care of themselves in the wild. We do the best we can to give them a good and healthy life while supporting the preservation of their natural habitats."

Victoria stopped in front of a wood and metal fence. Beyond the fence was a grassy open area with the occasional stand of trees and watering holes. "This is our savanna area," she told them. "We have several species of antelope and deer here. And something else. Do you see them?"

"Zebras," the twins cried. The striped animals grazed happily along with the other hoofed savanna creatures.

Sophie tugged at her grandmother's arm. "Will you take a picture of us?"

Harriet smiled as the twins looped their arms around each other and beamed and Aunt Jinny snapped a photo on her phone.

Victoria took them through the entire zoo, with stops to see a very old and dignified male lion named Regis, the monkey and marmoset house, exotic birds such as ostriches, a reptile house, and another of the collection's highlights, an elephant named Peanut.

"I can't believe how big he is," Sophie said, craning her neck.

"You say that every time," Sebastian pointed out.

Sophie crossed her arms. "Well, he doesn't get any smaller." The adults exchanged smiles behind Sophie's back.

After admiring Peanut for a while, his every move a source of fascination, the group looped around to finish the tour. The last stop was the petting zoo, where sheep, rabbits, goats, and a pony were happy to see visitors. Sophie and Sebastian even got to feed the animals snacks. And then it was time to go.

Victoria walked them back to the Land Rover. "It was so nice to meet you, Harriet." She nodded to Aunt Jinny and the twins. "And to see you again. I'll keep you posted on how Mango is doing."

"Please do," Harriet said. "It was wonderful to meet you as well. I really enjoyed the tour."

"Anytime," Victoria said. "You never know. I might be calling you." She smiled at Jason. "Since this one insists on going on vacation."

"I know. I'm an embarrassment to my field," Jason said, not sounding the least bit embarrassed.

Harriet had the feeling that something might be brewing between Victoria and Jason. The way they looked at each other, the little jokes they shared. They had a lot in common too. What could be more natural?

As Aunt Jinny loaded the kids into the Beast, Harriet said to Jason, "What are the next steps in the investigation about Mango? Do you know?"

"The Wildlife Crimes Unit will be contacting the Bahamian government about how to proceed. They'll also be notifying local police units and Border Force agents to keep an eye out for other animals from the Caribbean. There have been a lot of reptiles smuggled from that region, so one area of focus is an upcoming reptile-enthusiasts show in York." Jason pulled out his phone. "I'll send you a link. Smuggled reptiles were discovered during a recent show in Germany. That led to a big crackdown."

Harriet felt a leap of excitement. "Do you think I should go?" While there appeared to be plenty of law enforcement entities involved already—local police, Border Force, the Wildlife Crimes Unit—she liked the idea of playing a part, no matter how small, in righting this wrong.

"Give it some thought," Jason said, still busy with his phone. "As a vet, you'd be another pair of expert eyes to identify and combat animal smuggling. Maybe ask questions when someone brings a pet into your clinic. Subscribe to bulletins about smuggling cases. That kind of thing."

Harriet's phone pinged with his text. "Got it." She thought back over the patients she'd seen. "I haven't encountered anything suspicious yet. Except for Mango, of course." Although she'd been aware that animal smuggling existed, it hadn't been on her radar before.

But it sure was now.

Gulls swooped and cried as Harriet, Will, and Polly made their way along a cobblestone street toward the waterfront. Whitby, a charming jumble of whitewashed buildings with red roofs, sprawled on both sides of the harbor as if keeping guard. An abbey, a lighthouse, and a great mix of restaurants and shops made the town a popular destination. Even on this March Sunday afternoon, there were plenty of people out and about.

"Just what the doctor ordered," Will said, a twinkle in his hazel eyes. "This brisk sea air will clear out the cobwebs for sure." Sporting a red anorak, jeans, and a wool cap snug over his graying brown hair, Will was far more casual than he had been a couple of hours earlier while leading the service at White Church. Harriet thought he was equally handsome in both guises.

A strong gust whipped up the narrow lane. "There go the rest of my cobwebs," she said with a laugh.

Polly shivered, pulling her pink beanie lower over her ears. "I hope I dressed warmly enough."

"I have an extra sweater," Harriet said. Growing up in New England with its temperamental weather, she'd learned to be well prepared. And to wear layers.

"I might take you up on that," Polly said. "Which dock is it, Will?"

He pointed to one of a series of floating docks along the harbor's edge. "That one. See the yellow sign?"

Polly started walking faster. "I also see other people lining up. I hope we're not late."

Will checked his watch. "Fifteen minutes before launch. We're fine."

While Harriet hadn't expected a private boat tour, she was surprised at the number of people waiting to board. The double-decked boat, painted yellow like the sign, looked like it had room for about thirty, and Harriet guessed they would have a full roster.

They descended a wide, floating gangway to reach the dock just as Captain Ezra opened the passenger gate. "We're ready to board," he called out in a deep voice. With his thick beard, stocky build, and friendly features, he was made for the role of hearty sea captain.

"Get in line, please, and easy as you go. Don't want anyone falling into the drink. It's too early for a man overboard drill."

Everyone laughed.

Running footsteps sounded behind them, and Harriet glanced over her shoulder at the latecomer.

Van? Had Polly invited him? No, Polly looked as surprised as Harriet felt. Had it been Will? Perhaps a tactless move under the circumstances.

"Hello, Van," Will said, shaking his friend's hand. "I didn't know you'd be joining us today." So this was news to him as well.

"Someone told me about the tour, and I booked a ticket." He slid a glance toward Polly. "Had no idea you all would be here."

"Good to see you," Harriet said, her voice a little too jolly even to her own ears. "It's a lovely day for a boat ride, don't you think?" She liked Van and welcomed his company. It was Polly she was concerned about.

"Names, please." Captain Ezra's pen was poised to check them off. They each gave their name, and the captain made tick marks. "You're all set. Welcome aboard."

Harriet and Polly went through the gate, Van and Will chatting behind them. "Are you okay with this?" Harriet whispered to Polly. Her friend and the detective constable had decided to be friends, but there was a difference between that and being comfortable confined on a boat together.

Polly nodded. "Have to be, I suppose. Want to stand by the rail over there?" She pointed.

"Sure." Harriet wanted to be in a position to see everything. She'd mostly observed the ocean from shore until today, when she'd get to enjoy the reverse. She shrugged out of her small backpack and pulled a pair of binoculars from it.

"Great idea to bring those," Polly said. "I wish I had."

"We can share." Harriet settled the strap around her neck.

As the men joined them, the boat let out a huge blast, a signal that they were about to embark. The engines rumbled, and the craft began to ease away from the dock.

Excitement grew in Harriet's chest, and she grinned. "I love boat rides."

"So do I." Will stood on one side of Harriet, Polly on the other. Van was beside Will.

As the tour boat eased through the harbor, the loudspeaker crackled into life. "Good afternoon, everyone. Welcome to the inaugural voyage of the *Whitby Queen* for the new season. Every year we like to do a so-called 'dry run'"—Captain Ezra paused for laughs—"to make sure the old gal is still seaworthy."

Another pause, but this time the passengers were shocked into silence.

"Thank you for your feedback. I won't tell that joke on future tours. We spend the down months going over every inch of the *Queen*, removing barnacles, making repairs and improvements, and giving her a fresh coat of paint. This voyage is to get the barnacles off our operations, make sure the refreshment service operates smoothly, and, most of all, make sure I'm not mutinied by the crew or the guests."

The passengers laughed again, relief clear in the sound.

"I won't be talking the whole time, in case you're worried. I'll merely be pointing out sites of interest so you don't miss anything important. Sit back, relax, and enjoy the tour."

"Thanks for the reassurances, Captain," someone called, making people chuckle.

Captain Ezra gave a thumbs-up, indicating he'd heard.

The boat traveled through the narrow harbor mouth, flanked by lighthouses, and into open water, where it picked up speed. A wake formed along the sides of the boat, and a strong breeze tugged at hats and loose clothing.

Several seats were available nearby, so Harriet moved to one and set her pack down. The others joined her. "Cup of tea, anyone?" Harriet had brought a large flask to share. Only three cups though.

"I'll nip inside and get my own," Van said, eyeing the cups. "Be right back."

Polly wrapped her arms around her middle with a shiver. "I'll take that extra sweater, if you don't mind."

"Not at all." Harriet extracted the garment from the pack and handed it over.

To her surprise, Polly got up and started moving toward the cabin instead of putting the sweater on right there.

"Maybe she wants to talk to Van," Will said.

"Maybe." Harriet poured tea into a cup and handed it to him, then she filled another. "Cheers."

"Cheers." Will touched his cup to hers.

They sipped tea, listening to Captain Ezra. "Hild, the daughter of an Anglican nobleman, founded Whitby Abbey in the year 657." He added facts about the abbey's history, including its dissolution under Henry VIII and the fact that the ruins were still used as a landmark by sailors.

Harriet whistled under her breath. "Over thirteen hundred years old. That's amazing." She was often awed by the history all around her in England.

"They built things to last," Will said. "It's quite humbling to reflect on being a pastor in such a long tradition of service in Yorkshire."

"Which you do beautifully," Harriet said. "I know how you feel, sort of. I'm only the third generation of vets at Cobble Hill though."

He took her hand. "Both an honor and a challenge, isn't it?"

"Exactly." Harriet appreciated how she could share thoughts and feelings so easily with Will. He accepted her for who she was, and she considered that a profound gift of their relationship.

"We're approaching Saltwick Bay, ladies and gents," Captain Ezra announced through the loudspeaker. "This part of the coast is famous for several reasons, including alum mines, fossils, and shipwrecks. What is alum, you ask? It's a mineral compound that was used to make dyed cloth colorfast, as well as for many other things. We'd been cut off from our Italian supply by King Henry VIII's break from the Catholic Church, so we needed a new source."

They were now cruising fairly close to shore. Captain Ezra spoke about the fossils found in the bay. He explained that fossil hunting was allowed, although breaking up rocks was not.

Someone standing at the rail pointed, calling, "I see a shipwreck."

Harriet and Will hurried to the rail to see for themselves.

"As I said, folks," Captain Ezra said, "Saltwick Bay is known as a dangerous spot for ships, and when the tide is right, you can view a number of shipwrecks, many run aground on the bay island of Black Nab."

Pieces of ships came into view, submerged in the sea bottom with hull timbers and metal pieces showing. Van and Polly emerged from the cabin and joined Will and Harriet, who had found places at the rail.

"You can see trawlers, a hospital ship from the First World War, and cargo vessels," Captain Ezra said.

"How about a sailboat?" asked a man standing near Harriet.

Harriet followed his gesture to a red hull and a broken mast partially covered by water. A yacht bell chimed as the water washed over it.

"That's the *Petrel*," another man exclaimed. "Right color, right size. No other boats of that description have gone down along here." Others in the crowd picked up the idea, and excited voices began to buzz.

"What's the big deal?" Harriet asked Polly quietly.

Polly bit her lip. "The *Petrel* is the boat that belonged to Victoria Langford's brother. It went down twenty years ago and was never found."

CHAPTER FIVE

Van handed his tea to Polly and dodged through the crowd. A moment later, they saw him on the bridge talking to Captain Ezra. The boat's powerful engines began to reverse, with the effect that the craft was held in place.

This development caused an even greater uproar among the passengers. "Surely they're not going to retrieve it now," an older woman cried out.

"Of course not," a man standing near her said. "They need to get the coordinates so they can do that later."

"Why would the boat be visible now?" Harriet asked Will.

He shrugged. "The ocean bottom is always changing. The wreck might have been pushed in from deeper water during a storm. As the Scriptures say, 'For there is nothing hidden that will not be disclosed and nothing concealed that will not be known or brought out into the open.' Never truer than when it comes to the sea." He paused. "Or human nature."

"You're right about that." Harriet's heart ached for Victoria. While this discovery might bring her closure, it was also sure to open old wounds.

The loudspeaker crackled, and Van spoke. "Sorry for the delay, everyone. We have to mark the sailboat wreck while we can see it. A retrieval crew might not be able to get here until tomorrow. Our task will take a little while, so tea and biscuits are on the house, thanks to the captain."

This announcement caused a surge of movement toward the enclosed cabin, where the refreshments were sold. Harriet stood transfixed at the rail. Hopefully, the police would contact Victoria quickly, before news of this discovery reached social media. Judging by the number of phones she saw pointed at the wreck, it might already be too late.

Soon, an inflatable craft was lowered with Van and a mate aboard. They motored over to the area then tied a buoy to the largest piece of wreckage. Now the retrieval team would be able to easily spot the ruins of the *Petrel*.

The inflatable returned to the *Queen*, and Van and the mate climbed aboard. Van again went up to the bridge, likely to talk to the captain and make contact with the coast guard and other authorities.

Engines grumbled, and the boat continued on its way. Harriet wondered if the rest of the tour would be canceled. No doubt it would have been if the wreck had been recent or they'd actually witnessed people in danger. Twenty years later, there wasn't much that could be done, except mourn the dead.

Captain Ezra did make a few half-hearted attempts with his spiel but soon abandoned them. Not that the passengers seemed unhappy. They were still excited about the discovery, chatting about it while enjoying their snacks.

"Are you all right?" Will asked Harriet. "You're awfully quiet."

"I'm stunned and sad," she admitted. "After meeting Victoria yesterday, I can't help thinking of how this will affect her."

"That's understandable," he said. "It's tragic that two young men lost their lives this way. They were only eighteen, I believe?"

Polly nodded. "About to start university. I was a kid when it happened, but I remember afterwards that my parents warned us all the time about keeping an eye on the weather when we went boating. Storms can spring up suddenly, sometimes out of nowhere."

"This section of coast has had many shipwrecks," Will said. "Look at all the memorials at the church." As a fishing community, White Church Bay had endured its share of sailors lost at sea, not to mention the foundering of ships passing by.

Another engine buzzed on the bay, heading directly toward the tour boat. Again, the captain cut the engines, and the coast guard craft drew alongside. Van climbed aboard, and they continued on to the shipwreck.

"It's a good thing Van was here," Polly said. "He really took charge, didn't he?" Admiration shone in her eyes.

"We're lucky to have him in White Church Bay," Will agreed. "He's a talented officer, not to mention a thoroughly decent man."

Polly gazed thoughtfully at the passing scenery, and Harriet wondered if her friend was having second thoughts about the breakup. If they ended up together, this time apart might have been a necessary test of their relationship, painful as it had been.

Harriet had to give Polly points for not taking the path of least resistance. She knew too many people who had been swept away by romance, married too soon, and regretted it. It took fortitude and self-awareness for someone to say, *Hold on, I'm not ready*, especially when it hurt to do so.

The tour boat reached White Church Bay, and Captain Ezra pointed out a few highlights, mentioning the long history of smuggling in the area. Nowadays more than European goods were brought in illicitly.

Last night, Harriet had researched wildlife crime in the UK and worldwide and had been stunned at the sheer volume of animals smuggled and sold on the black market. Moorland Zoo was the result of a fascination with God's varied creation, and that interest wasn't confined to gazing at animals in a zoo. Some people took it a step further, to actually owning them.

She was sure many didn't realize what they were signing up for, and as a result, the pets suffered. Mango was a good example. She came from a warm climate, and caring for her properly required a large space that mimicked her natural habitat as closely as possible.

With the iguana's requirements, it was fortunate Victoria had taken Mango in until the agency could decide the next steps. Yesterday, after returning from the zoo, Harriet and her family had spent a couple of hours scouring Cobble Hill Farm for additional iguanas. They'd focused on rock walls and other areas where the creatures might hide. The hunt had been unsuccessful, and Harriet prayed they hadn't missed any, especially with night temperatures hovering around freezing.

"Will you go see Victoria Langford?" she asked Will. As a pastor, he provided comfort and support to the bereaved.

"I'll give her a call once we're on shore. Langford Hall is in my parish, although barely. The family often goes to a different church out of convenience, but I officiated at her father's funeral."

He was acquainted with Victoria then. That eased Harriet's mind. She'd seen him in action and had experienced his extraordinary compassion and wisdom herself.

The *Queen* circled around and headed back up the coast to Whitby. As they approached Saltwick Bay, anticipation gripped the passengers. Harriet was interested as well to see what was going on at the shipwreck site.

Several boats clustered near the *Petrel*, the ebbing tide requiring caution. A couple of inflatables were at the wreck, able to approach with their shallow draft.

"They're probably doing a formal identification of the sailboat," Polly said. "Although it's pretty clear that it's the *Petrel*. There's Van." She waved at the men and women wearing bright vests and waterproofs.

Harriet couldn't tell which one was Van. "I'll take your word for it." Then one of the figures waved back, and Polly broke into a big smile. *Even at a distance, some hearts recognize each other.* Harriet kept the romantic thought to herself.

The loudspeaker crackled. "Let's have a moment of silence, folks," Captain Ezra said. "For the dearly departed lost to the sea."

The passengers complied, some bowing their heads while others gazed at the wreck as if honoring the victims. Danger on the sea was never far, even in modern times. Despite the best instruments, forecasting, and building materials, the weather and waves could still swamp and sink vessels.

Polly blinked, her face scrunched against the wind. "It's so sad."

"It is," Harriet agreed. Two young lives cut off far too soon. If there was any peace or closure to be had from the tragedy, Harriet meant to find it for Victoria's sake.

"Care for some tea at the Happy Cup?" Will asked as they disembarked from the *Queen*. "I'm too restless to head home." Despite checking their phones frequently, none of the three had heard from Van yet.

"I'd love to," Harriet said. "What about you, Polly?"

"Sounds good." Polly shivered as they walked up the dock toward the street. "I'm chilled to the bone."

"Even with my sweater?" Harriet asked.

Her assistant rubbed her arms. "This chill goes beyond clothing."

Considering the hollow, cold sensation in her own core, Harriet understood her meaning. Coming upon the sailboat had been a shock almost as severe as if it had just sunk. A terrible reminder of mortality.

Back in White Church Bay, Will parked his Kia at the rectory, an easy walk from the Happy Cup Tearoom and Bakery. "I'll be happy to run you home later," he told Harriet.

"Thanks," Harriet said. "That'll depend on how many tea cakes I eat." She'd either want to walk them off or be so full and content that she couldn't bring herself to trudge home in the cold.

White Church Bay was a popular tourist destination, even on a Sunday in March, and people were strolling the lanes and streaming in and out of shops and restaurants. The Happy Cup, with its pale green frontage, valance, and spring-themed window display, was as cozy and welcoming as ever.

The trio stepped inside, greeted by the aroma of tea, coffee, and baked goods. Most of the tables were full, and servers bustled back and forth with trays.

"There's a table," Polly said. "Better grab it before someone else does."

They hastily made their way to the spot. After taking off their coats, they sat down and picked up the menus set on each place mat.

"I'm kind of hungry," Will said. "I might go for a sandwich platter, if you two would like to share." The platter offered assorted sandwiches, including smoked salmon, cucumber, ham, tuna, and curried chicken.

"I'll eat one or two," Harriet said. Everything at the Happy Cup was good.

"So will I," Polly said. "How about a plate of mini pastries to go with it?" The plate included small cream puffs, scones, cakes, and tarts.

"Perfect," Harriet said.

A woman with a long auburn braid approached the table. "Good afternoon. Welcome to the Happy Cup." As the server placed a glass of water and a bundle of silverware at each setting, Harriet recognized her. She'd been at the protest outside the zoo.

The server straightened, her gaze falling on Harriet. "You're the vet."

Harriet smiled. "I am. Dr. Harriet Bailey." Waving at her companions, she added, "This is my assistant, Polly Thatcher, and Pastor Will Knight."

"Ruth Armstrong," the woman replied.

"You must be new here," Polly said. "Keri Stone is usually working." Keri also served as the church webmaster.

Ruth smiled. "She still works here, but she's been so busy with her web business that they hired me to pick up a few shifts." She pulled a pad and pencil out of her apron pocket, took their order, then hurried away.

"What was that all about?" Polly asked.

Harriet filled them in on her first meeting with Ruth. "She didn't seem all that thrilled to see me again."

"You're the enemy," Will said. "A zoo supporter."

"I probably am, in her mind." Pushing the uncomfortable topic aside, Harriet asked Will, "Have you heard from Van?"

Will checked his phone. "Not yet." He continued to scroll. "Nothing's hit the news yet either."

"Good," Polly said. "Victoria doesn't need to hear about it that way."

Ruth bustled up to the next table, where Agnes Galloway, owner of a local general store, sat with her husband, Gavin.

"This looks delicious," Agnes said as Ruth set a sandwich in front of her. "Tell me again where you went on your last trip." To Gavin, she said, "Ruth is quite the world traveler."

"Not exactly." Ruth chuckled as she placed another plate in front of Gavin. "I was in Germany and Switzerland for a week. Once I get a full-time position, there won't be any more gallivanting for me." She placed individual teapots on the table along with cups and a pitcher of milk.

"What kind of position are you looking for?" Gavin asked. Like his wife, he was gregarious and kind, always ready to help.

Ruth paused, empty tray under her arm. "Anything to do with animals, which is my passion. In my last job, I ran a shelter for cats and dogs outside London. Yorkshire's home, so I'd like to make a go of it here."

"I'll keep my ears open and let you know if I hear of anything," Gavin said.

"How nice," Ruth replied. "Thank you."

Harriet guessed Ruth wouldn't be approaching her for a job, not after the encounter at the zoo. Had she moved to the area specifically to oppose the Langford family's zoo? If so, why? Didn't she realize that she and Victoria were on the same side?

Perhaps sensing Harriet's gaze, Ruth turned. "Your order will be right up," she said briskly. Then she strode away.

"Obvious I was listening, huh?" Harriet sank lower in her chair.

"We all were," Polly said. "The tearoom isn't a place to discuss secrets, that's for sure." She grinned at Agnes. "Hello, Agnes, Gavin."

"Lovely to see you." Agnes's nod took in the entire table. "Beautiful Sunday afternoon, isn't it?"

They echoed agreement and exchanged a few pleasantries. Noticing Ruth on her way to Harriet's table with a tray, the Galloways turned to their meal.

The plates of sandwiches and baked goods were nearly demolished when Will's phone rang. "It's Van," he said. "I should get this."

"Please do," Harriet said, eager for an update on the shipwreck.

"Hello, Van," Will said. He listened intently for a moment. "In an hour? I'll be there."

Harriet and Polly stared at him expectantly as he disconnected the call.

"It is the *Petrel*, as we thought," Will said, his voice low and somber. "They discovered skeletal remains on board. A young male."

CHAPTER SIX

"Oh no," Harriet murmured. Although it had been widely accepted that two young men had drowned, discovering proof of it was still sad.

"They don't know which one it is, do they?" Polly asked.

"Not yet," Will replied. "I'm sure they'll investigate thoroughly and try to identify him."

"Nick was with his cousin, Scott, I understand," Harriet said. "Does Scott have parents or siblings?" How heart-wrenching the wait must be for both families.

"I don't know," Will said. "Van wants me to meet him at the Langford home in an hour to talk to Victoria. Would you like to come with me? She might appreciate a feminine shoulder."

"Of course I will," Harriet said. "Polly, you should come too. You're great in these situations."

Polly gave her a small smile. "I'm glad you think so. I'll do anything I can to help. Poor Victoria. My heart goes out to her."

Harriet felt the same way.

Harriet and Polly rode in the Beast to Langford Hall, and Will drove his own car. Thanks to Will's coordination with Van, the detective constable arrived as they pulled through the open gates.

"I gave Victoria a heads-up we were coming," Van said as they convened in the parking lot. "I told her there was news concerning her brother's accident." Smartly dressed in a neatly pressed uniform, Van conveyed both competence and kindness.

If I had to hear bad news, Harriet thought, *I'd want Van to deliver it.*

With Van in the lead, they made their way through the hedge and along the path to the rear entrance. In the distance, an animal roared, joined by the raucous cry of a peacock and the chatter of monkeys.

"Sounds like a jungle out there," Van said. "Was that a lion?"

"I think so, yes," Will said. He glanced around, as if half-expecting it to come bounding out of the bushes.

"Don't worry," Harriet said. "He's safely caged."

Victoria answered immediately when Van thumped the door knocker. "Thanks for coming," she said, her gaze sweeping over the little group. "I appreciate the support." Despite her air of composure, Harriet noticed that her hands trembled, revealing her trepidation.

Van removed his hat, holding it to his chest as he said, "Could we come in, please? As I told you on the phone, I have some news to discuss with you."

"Of course," Victoria said. "Let's go through to the drawing room. I was just having my tea in there."

They passed the door to the conservatory, and Harriet decided to request a peek at Mango later. She would take a picture and send it to the twins' father, knowing Sebastian and Sophie would love the update.

Harriet gazed around with interest as they made their way to the drawing room at the front of the manor. Portraits and paintings lined the corridor walls, and the entrance hall reminded her of medieval days with its beamed ceilings and suits of armor. "What a beautiful home you have, Victoria."

"This place? It's ancient," Victoria said with a laugh. "The Langfords have been here forever. Here we are." She ushered them through a pair of open double doors and into a gracious room with high ceilings and groupings of brocade upholstered furniture. "Now, what's going on?"

Van stood a little straighter, shoulders back. "Miss Langford, we have news about your brother's boat, the *Petrel*."

Victoria, who had been standing near the fireplace mantel, gripped it as if to steady herself. "Has it finally been found?"

"Yes, earlier today near Saltwick Bay. The craft was spotted from a tour boat traversing the area. Upon closer examination, we were able to confirm its identity."

When Victoria swayed on her feet, Will hurried to her side, offering a supportive hand under her elbow. "Why don't you sit down?" he suggested, guiding her to a nearby armchair.

After their hostess sat, Harriet and Polly took seats on a sofa. Van remained standing, and Will hovered near Victoria's chair.

Victoria licked her lips. "There's more, isn't there? I can tell." She spoke in a monotone, all emotion suppressed behind a rigid facade.

"I'm afraid so, Miss Langford," Van said. "Once the sailboat was pulled from the muck, the skeletal remains of a young man were found aboard."

The young woman's controlled facade shattered. Putting a fist to her mouth, Victoria made a terrible choking sound.

Harriet sprang to her feet. "I'll get you some water," she murmured, hurrying toward the door.

Polly also got up, retrieving a box of tissues and putting them on an end table within reach. "There, there, love. Let it out."

Loud sobs followed Harriet as she raced down the corridor.

In the kitchen, she flipped doors open, searching for glasses. She finally found one and filled it with cold water from the sink. Then as she started to rush back, she came to a sliding stop. Maybe she should make a strong cup of tea with sugar, the traditional remedy for shock.

Then she jolted into action again. Victoria said she'd been having tea in the drawing room.

When she rejoined the others, Victoria was sipping at a cup. "Oh, good," Harriet said, setting the glass on a coaster.

"You're all wonderful," Victoria said, tears still shining in her eyes. "I can't thank you enough for your support."

Polly left the room and returned moments later with more teacups. Then she poured tea for everyone.

When her guests were settled, Victoria said, "I was five years old the night my brother and my cousin disappeared. My father was hosting a party here that night, which served to make things more confusing. I remember that Nick argued with Dad and then left in a huff with Scott."

Harriet winced. She couldn't imagine how that must have weighed on Marshall Langford.

"My next memory is of later that night, with the huge thunderstorm that came through. There were tents in the garden, but everyone ran inside, soaking wet and laughing. Until the phone rang. Someone had seen the *Petrel* struggling in the water."

Sitting here at Langford Hall, Harriet could easily picture the scene.

"Dad immediately called the Coast Guard and the police, insisting that a search party be launched." White Church Bay, like all coastal towns, had its own lifeboat service staffed by volunteers. "Everything had to wait until the storm quieted down. They had a vague idea of where the sailboat might be, from what the witness told them."

"Who was the witness?" Van asked. "Do you remember?"

Victoria nodded. "She was a good friend of Nick's. A girl named Ruth Armstrong."

Harriet and her friends looked at each other. "Does she have red hair?" Harriet asked.

"She does." Victoria sounded eager. "Do you know her?"

Harriet debated whether to mention the protest. She decided to go ahead, in case Ruth showed up again. She didn't want Victoria to be blindsided.

"Actually, I first met her outside your gates," Harriet said. "She was one of the protestors. I didn't know her name then. Then we ran into her at the Happy Cup just before we came here. She's working there as a server."

Victoria absorbed her words, expression unreadable. "Interesting. Ruth was always fascinated by the zoo. She even worked here a couple of summers. And now she's protesting us?"

"She's still working with animals," Will said. "Actually, she's hunting for a job in that field right now."

Van rubbed his chin. "A friend of Nick's, you say. Was she at the party?"

Victoria shrugged. "I assume so. She was always hanging around the boys. Part of their gang."

"I'm going to dig through the archives and see what we have on the incident," Van said. "Maybe I'll talk to Miss Armstrong and see if she remembers anything else about that night."

"I appreciate that, Detective Constable," Victoria said. "Any answers will help, although nothing will bring my brother back." She dabbed at her eyes. "My father had a hard time accepting his death. For years, we hoped he would come home one day and help run the estate and the zoo. Nick and I were supposed to share everything, fifty-fifty."

Harriet sympathized with Victoria's father. While Nick's body was missing, there was still hope.

"It's heartbreaking for sure," Polly said. "Would you like another cup of tea?"

"If there's any left."

"I think so, yes. If not, I'll be happy to brew another pot." Polly brought the teapot over and filled Victoria's cup then provided milk and sugar in turn.

Van watched Polly, hastily ducking his head when she looked his way.

"How long do you think it will take?" Victoria asked. "The identification, I mean?"

"Depends on several factors," Van said. "If we have dental records, it will be fairly straightforward. Otherwise, there's DNA testing, but I'm afraid that can take a while."

"If you need a sample, I'm more than happy to provide one." Victoria clasped her hands together. "There's a possibility that it might be Scott, right? Not that I want it to be either of them, but it's likely to be one or the other."

Harriet hoped they would be able to use dental records. Otherwise, Victoria would be on pins and needles waiting for the lab to make a determination. She deserved peace after decades of not knowing, not more waiting.

The doorbell sounded, a deep, sonorous bong. Victoria started to put her cup down, but Harriet sprang to her feet. "I'll go. You sit back and relax."

"It might be someone from the department," Van said. "I'll go with you."

From prior experience with local law enforcement, Harriet knew that major crimes and incidents were handled by a district office. Anything that was deemed above Van's authority level was passed up to his superiors.

The doorbell rang again as Harriet and Van crossed the entrance hall. "This is the worst part of the job," Van said in a low voice. "Telling the family bad news about a loved one."

"I can imagine," Harriet said. "You handled it well."

His cheeks flushed slightly. "Good of you to say."

They arrived at the double front door, a massive, carved affair, and Harriet turned the knob, admiring how smoothly the panel opened, without a creak.

Two men stood on the step. One was of medium height with dark hair cut short and sweeping across his brow. He was handsome and restless, foot tapping, hands jingling coins in his pocket. The other man was taller and larger, with close-cropped blond hair and pale blue eyes. He wore a crooked grin and an air of expectant good humor.

"Can I help you?" Harriet asked.

Both men looked taken aback to see a policeman standing next to Harriet. After a hesitant moment, the dark-haired man said, "I'm Nick Langford. Is my sister at home?"

CHAPTER SEVEN

Harriet felt her mouth drop open. "Nick Langford?" she finally managed to spit out. "I thought you were—"

"Dead?" His green eyes glowed with grim amusement. "I'm not, as you can see." He made an ushering motion. "Step aside, please. I'd like to come in."

Van put up a hand. "Hold on, sir. Identification, please."

"Are you serious, mate?" the blond man demanded in a thick Australian accent. "This is his ancestral home."

The detective constable appeared unmoved as he folded his arms. "So you say. We'll need verification on that."

The man claiming to be Nick made a scoffing sound. "Go get my sister. She'll vouch for me."

"I hope so," Harriet said. "If this is a trick, I'll have your head. She's already upset enough."

The two men glanced at each other. "Yeah, we heard," the blond man said. "Odd timing, isn't it? Finding the sailboat, I mean."

The same day Nick showed his face after twenty years. Although Harriet didn't believe he was an impostor—such a feat was difficult if not impossible to pull off nowadays—she still felt they should err on the side of caution. Even if it was Nick, it was Victoria's decision whether or not she allowed him into her home. Or was it her home?

She had said the estate was to be split between her and Nick. Would his return change things? Would he claim his share?

"Van, why don't you wait here, and I'll get Victoria?" Harriet suggested.

"Go ahead. I'll keep an eye on them." Van adjusted his stance, daring the men to try to push past him.

Harriet ran to the drawing room, her heart pounding.

Only minutes ago, Victoria had been consumed with grief over the loss of her brother. Now he was here, at Langford Hall. Where had he been all these years? Why had he come back? Why hadn't he returned while his father was alive? The poor man had died grieving his son.

The whole thing left a bad taste in Harriet's mouth.

With a jolt of remorse, she remembered that it wasn't her place to judge. She didn't know anything about the history between Nick and his father. After all, she'd just met Victoria, and though she liked her, the young woman had been a child when the tragedy occurred. Her memories and insights might not be especially accurate.

When Harriet halted in the drawing room doorway, Will took one look at her and got to his feet. "What is it? You seem upset."

Harriet drew in a deep breath. "Victoria, a man claiming to be Nick is here."

Victoria shook her head, obviously bewildered. "Did you say Nick is here? Are you sure?"

"He says he's your brother." Harriet gestured. "Please come see. Van is guarding the door and won't let him in until you say it's okay."

Will went to Victoria and held out a hand. "I'll go with you."

Victoria placed her hand in his, and he helped her rise. He escorted her from the drawing room, Harriet and Polly right behind them.

"This is incredible," Polly whispered to Harriet. "Do you think it's really him?"

Harriet shook her head. "I have no idea."

Victoria gave a shriek when she saw the men standing on the front steps. "Nick? Is it really you?"

"It's me, pumpkin." He rolled up his sleeve. "See the scar from when the goat bit me?" He pointed to a faint line on his tanned forearm.

"I remember that story," Victoria said.

He stared into her face as if memorizing every detail. "You're all grown up."

"What did you expect?" Victoria said. "It's been twenty years. Oh, Nick. Where did you go?" She began to cry again, this time happy tears.

If Nick was here, he had survived the sailboat's sinking, and his remains weren't on the boat. They must belong to Scott, the Langfords' cousin. Why hadn't Nick returned home after the incident? Harriet had so many questions.

"I have a lot to tell you," Nick said. "But first, can you forgive me?" The young man's face was twisted with sorrow and regret. "I made a huge mistake. And then I couldn't figure out how to make things right."

"Of course I forgive you," Victoria said. "Please come in." She beamed through the tears as she took Nick's arm.

"This is my friend, Ozzie Bright. Ozzie, my sister, Victoria."

Ozzie grinned. "Nice to meet you. Lovely place you have here."

Will gestured to Harriet and the others. "I think this is our cue to leave. Let Nick get settled and reacquainted with his sister." They nodded in agreement, and Will said, "Welcome home, Nick. We'll see you later, Victoria."

"Really? You're leaving?" Victoria turned to her brother. "Nick, say hello to my friends." She went around the circle and introduced everyone.

"Is it all right if I take a peek at Mango before we go?" Harriet asked.

"Please," Victoria said. "She's doing really well."

"We can show ourselves out," Van said to Victoria. "We don't want to keep you from your guests. If you need anything, you can call me anytime."

"Thank you, DC Worthington," Victoria said. "I can't thank you enough for all you've done. All of you." With a last beaming smile, she ushered Nick and Ozzie into the drawing room.

Harriet led her friends to the conservatory. She went over to the cage, phone ready to take a picture. Will followed her, close on her heels. He hadn't seen the iguana yet, and he was fascinated.

Harriet crouched beside the cage and easily spotted the iguana. "The twins are going to love seeing this," she said as she snapped a shot.

"Can they keep her?" Will asked.

"I'm afraid not." Harriet sent a text to Anthony, attaching the photo. "She's rare and endangered. She'll be flying home once officials make the arrangements. A one-way ticket to the Bahamas."

"I could use one of those myself," Polly joked.

Harriet rested her hands on her hips in mock outrage. "You'd better come back. I need you."

Polly laughed. "Okay, a round-trip ticket. Seriously, though, I've always wanted to travel to the Caribbean."

So had Harriet. But right now, she was far too busy to even think about a vacation. And she was good with that. She loved her life, especially when it was full of happy endings.

The next morning at the clinic, the *Petrel*, the skeleton, and Nick Langford's return were all anyone could talk about.

"I heard you were there when they found the sailboat," Jane Birtwhistle said. Jane was one of the clinic's regular customers, with several cats in her care. She was a sweet older woman, and Harriet was always glad to see her.

Harriet placed Pumpkin, a plump orange cat, on the scales. The cat's name reminded her of Victoria. Nick had called her pumpkin. Not that Victoria and her family situation had been far from her thoughts today, with all the questions and speculations.

"I was," Harriet said. "I'd never heard of the *Petrel*. It was other passengers who identified it."

"I remember that storm," Jane said. "It came up so fast, thunder and lightning and high winds. The cats ran to hide under the beds, poor things, when thunder shook the house. Then a big branch from a tree came down and barely missed my roof."

"Phew. Glad it missed." Harriet checked Pumpkin's other vitals. Other than his weight, he was strong and healthy.

"Me too. There was a lot of storm damage all around. And then the report came in that a boat had gone down. Someone saw it struggling in the water, almost capsizing."

That matched what Victoria had said. Harriet paused her tasks, gripped by the awful image. "Then you heard it was the *Petrel*?"

"Someone reported it to the coast guard and the lifeboat service. By the time they could get anywhere near it, it was gone. Sunk without a trace." Jane's expression was bleak. "A too-familiar story in these waters."

Harriet wondered if Jane had lost someone to the sea. So many in White Church Bay had, whether family or friends or neighbors.

"Is there any news about the remains they found?" Jane asked. "I understand they think it was Scott Spencer?"

"I haven't heard anything," Harriet said. "Not that they would necessarily tell me."

"Those boys were quite the pair," Jane said. "Always rampaging around the village. It was all in good fun. They were full of high spirits and hijinks, like most young ones."

Harriet turned the discussion to Pumpkin, telling Jane that he was in great shape. His owner needed to make sure he didn't overeat though.

"Unlike Mittens," Jane said. "He had trouble gaining weight until you helped him. He's nice and sleek now."

Harriet had treated hyperthyroidism in the twelve-year-old cat. "I'm glad he's doing well."

Jane soon bustled out, cooing over Pumpkin in his carrier. Harriet had offered to carry it, but Jane insisted.

"Who's next?" Harriet asked Polly at the front desk. The waiting room still held three or four people. Once those pets were taken care of, they'd break for lunch.

"Cassandra Willis," Polly said. "She's here with Butterscotch, who needs a checkup."

Harriet went over to the pair. "Cassandra? I'm Dr. Harriet Bailey."

"Lovely to meet you." Cassandra was blond and elegant, dressed in sleek slacks and a blouse. Her fine wool coat was neatly draped over an adjacent chair. She bent to pick up the cat carrier. "This is Butterscotch."

"She's a Bengal," Harriet said in surprise. A hybrid mix of wild and domestic cats, Bengals had golden fur marked with spots. They also were very expensive.

"Isn't she gorgeous?" Cassandra cooed. "When I saw the litter, I just had to have one."

"Don't blame you a bit." Harriet gestured. "Please, follow me."

While Harriet examined the cat, who was friendly and inquisitive, Cassandra told her all about herself. After living in London, she'd recently moved back to the area and now lived in the "most adorable" cottage with an ocean view. Cassandra had a remote job in finance, which allowed her to purchase all kinds of goodies, including Butterscotch. Or so Harriet presumed. It also allowed her to travel frequently.

"I'm headed to the Caribbean next," Cassandra said. "Not sure exactly where yet. I might do a cruise to some of the more remote islands this time."

"That sounds wonderful." Harriet thought of Mango, who was from that area of the world.

"It will be," Cassandra said. "But home is best, isn't it?"

"I couldn't agree more," Harriet said. "Although I didn't grow up here, I visited often. I moved to England last year to take over my grandfather's practice."

"Yes, old Doc Bailey," Cassandra said. "I remember him from when I grew up here. He was a wonderful man."

This praise of her beloved grandfather warmed Harriet. "How nice of you to say. So you're a Yorkshire native?"

"That's right. I lived here until I went away to university. My parents moved soon after, to my grandparents' home in Norfolk. They're still there."

Since Cassandra had grown up locally, Harriet wondered if she'd known Nick Langford, but she didn't think she knew her well enough to ask.

But as it happened, she didn't have to ask. While Cassandra was coaxing Butterscotch back into the carrier, she asked, "Did you hear about the sailboat they found at Saltwick Bay?"

That was all she'd been hearing about today. "Actually, I was there when other passengers on the tour boat spotted it. Such a terrible tragedy."

Cassandra's eyes lit up. "There's good news though. Nick Langford has returned." She laughed. "Isn't that amazing? All that time, we thought he was dead." Her eyes grew distant. "We were part of the same crowd. Nick and I even dated for a while. We were kids back then, of course."

"Have you seen him yet?" Harriet asked. She assumed that Nick would be eager to see old friends and vice versa. Or perhaps not. He might wonder what kind of reception he would receive after disappearing the way he had. And his vanishing act still puzzled her. Why hadn't he raised the alarm when he made it to shore? Instead, he'd run away and ended up who knew where. She still hadn't heard those details.

Cassandra shook her head. "I'm sure he needs to settle in. I might put out feelers in a week or two, find out if he even wants to see me. It's been a long time. We've all changed. Grown up. Gone separate ways and lived separate lives."

"That sounds like a reasonable approach." Harriet made a final notation on Butterscotch's chart. "I'll walk you out."

When they reached the front desk, Polly said, "Dr. Peel on line one for you. Do you want to take it?"

"Yes," Harriet said. "It shouldn't take long." After waving goodbye to Cassandra, she went to the extension and picked up. "Hi, Jason. How are you?" Perhaps he had news about Mango. Not that she wanted her to leave, but the iguana needed to go home, to her own environment.

"I'm fine, thanks. Listen, Harriet, do you remember what we discussed? About you filling in for me?" He inhaled. "Well, I'm calling to see if you can do that this week. Just in north Yorkshire. I've got someone else who can cover the rest of the area."

Harriet thought over her schedule. No busier than usual but still relatively full. "How likely is it that I'll get a call? I want to make sure I have wiggle room."

"Totally understandable. Calls to your neck of the woods are quite rare, frankly. Mostly Moorland Zoo, which is my actual concern. I don't like leaving Victoria without someone to call on. She can handle the minor stuff herself, but if there's a real emergency or illness—"

"I understand. I'll do it. Exactly when are you going to be gone? Oh, and can I call you in case I need advice? Or other vets?"

He gave her the dates. "You can call or text me anytime. I'll also send you several names as backup. They're excellent folks."

"I appreciate it. Any news about Mango? Has a trip home been scheduled yet?"

"Hold on. Let me check my email." After a moment, he said, "I don't see anything from the Wildlife Crimes Unit. But I'm not coordinating. Border Force is."

"Maybe I'll check in with Darren Crosby. He's the agent in charge."

"Go ahead and do that, Harriet. Hopefully they'll get her returned soon."

"I think I will. You have a wonderful vacation."

Harriet hung up, hoping she wasn't making a terrible mistake. It wasn't the workload she was worried about. It was providing adequate care to species she'd never encountered before. Talk about being out of her comfort zone. With any luck, Grandad's journals would be able to help her rise to this new challenge.

CHAPTER EIGHT

Harriet's first call as an exotic vet came in that afternoon from Victoria Langford. "Harriet," she said, "I understand you're filling in for Jason Peel."

"I am as of today." She crossed her fingers that the request wouldn't be too complicated or involve procedures and techniques she'd have to research. "What do you need?"

"It's Zippy," Victoria said. "One of our zebras. He's managed to gash his leg, and I think it needs treatment. Not that he'll let me close enough to touch it."

Harriet had faced similar situations before, if not with this particular species, and she knew exactly what was needed. "I'll be out right after my last patient. Do you have a tranquilizer gun, or should I bring my own?" Holding the receiver with her shoulder, she brought up a web browser to search for the right sedative to use.

"We have a good inventory of tranquilizers," Victoria said. "Hold on. I'll go to the cupboard."

Victoria must have been out in the zoo, because it didn't take long for her to return to the line. "We're all set with those supplies."

"I'll see you in an hour or so," Harriet said, allowing time to change and drive out to the zoo.

"Let's meet at the entrance," Victoria said. "I'll be in the kiosk."

Polly sent Harriet a puzzled expression as she walked to the front of the clinic. "What's up?"

"Injured zebra over at Moorland Zoo. Want to come along?"

"You bet. I have my wellies and some old clothes in the boot."

After the final patient left, Harriet and Polly packed up supplies and equipment, changed, and jumped into the Land Rover.

"I feel like we're going on safari," Polly said. The afternoon was warm, so she had her elbow propped on the open window ledge.

"We kind of are." As Harriet navigated the winding roads, she mentally reviewed the treatment steps. It had been a while since she'd used a tranquilizer gun. Fortunately, she'd become an expert at treating lacerations.

The zoo gates were open, and Harriet parked as close to the kiosk as she could. Victoria popped out of the little building as they climbed from the vehicle.

"Thanks again for coming," she said. "Jason's been gone—what, a couple hours? And we already need you."

"Not a problem," Harriet said as she opened the rear to retrieve her bag. "Zippy, here we come."

They stopped by a service building on their way, where Victoria unlocked a closet, which turned out to be full of veterinary supplies. Harriet examined the tranquilizer gun and then loaded a syringe with solution. She wanted to handle the gun from start to finish, since she was trained.

As they strolled through the zoo, Harriet noticed Nick and Ozzie standing near the monkey cage, talking as they watched the primates play.

"You must be over the moon that your brother has come home," Polly said.

Victoria glanced toward the men. "I am. I have to pinch myself now and then to make sure I'm not dreaming."

"Is Nick going to help you with the zoo?" Harriet asked.

Victoria shrugged. "We haven't discussed it yet. I don't even know where he was all this time or why he ran away. He hasn't been ready to talk about it." Frustration laced her voice.

Was Nick still traumatized by the shipwreck? It was possible, even after twenty years, Harriet supposed. Especially if he'd witnessed his cousin's death.

"He hasn't told you where he was?" Polly sounded shocked. "That seems odd."

"I know a little," Victoria said. "Ozzie said they flew here from Cape Town. He told me they're partners in an export business. They work with arts and crafts from Africa and other parts of the world."

"Interesting." That part of the world was a draw for expats from everywhere, Harriet had gathered. Lots of sunshine, sailing, and a laid-back lifestyle.

"I'd like to see the arts and crafts," Polly said.

"Ozzie will probably tell you about them if you ask," Victoria said. "He's quite open, unlike my brother."

At Zippy's pen, Harriet used her binoculars to examine the animal. Focusing in, she could see a long cut down his rear left leg. He wasn't putting his full weight on it, which meant it must hurt. But she wouldn't be able to tell whether it was infected until she could see it up close.

Zippy was meandering around the enclosure, edging closer to an overhang at one end.

"I'll dart him when he goes under the shelter," Harriet said. "That's a good spot for him to be treated and rest until he wakes up." She took in the cloudy sky overhead. The last thing she wanted was for the zebra to get soaked with rain while lying on the ground.

The trio stood by the fence, waiting patiently for Zippy to reach the enclosure. When he finally walked under the roof, Harriet lifted the tranquilizer gun to her shoulder, sighted, and squeezed the trigger. Zippy staggered slightly, wandered a few more steps, and dropped.

"Wow," Polly exclaimed. "That was an amazing shot."

Harriet grinned. "I haven't done this for a while, so it might have been a lucky one."

They waited for a few minutes to be sure that Zippy was truly unconscious. Then Victoria unlocked the gate and they went into the enclosure. After donning protective gear, Harriet told the other two to stay back while she retrieved the dart. She then treated the injection site before gesturing for them to approach. The sedative used was so strong that it was dangerous for humans to touch it.

After donning fresh gloves, Harriet studied the injury. "Using stitches is a problem. This location requires the kind that won't absorb with time."

"Which means sedating him again to remove them later," Victoria said. "Can we get away without them?"

Harriet considered the injury. "Possibly. It's long, but it's not very deep. If we clean it and treat it to stave off infection, it might heal quickly by itself."

Polly knew the drill and had already opened the bag. The first step was to disinfect the wound, and she handed Harriet the correct supplies.

Victoria stood over them, watching as they worked. "I'd never guess this is your first zebra."

"I've taken care of a lot of horses," Harriet said. "If not for the stripes, I could believe that's what I'm treating now." She found the similarity comforting. Being asked to treat a truly unusual creature might be another story.

Conscious that the sedation would wear off soon, Harriet worked quickly. The last step was to take several pictures of the injury for reference. "I'll be back soon to check on him," she said. She would study the wound through binoculars to be sure it was healing. If it wasn't, they'd have to knock him out and treat him again. She hoped that wouldn't happen.

Once the task was complete, they hastily gathered their things and retreated from the enclosure. Soon Zippy began to stir, and after a false start or two, he lumbered to his feet. He took a few tentative steps, and it was soon apparent that his leg was already feeling better.

The three women cheered at the sight.

"Refreshments at the house before you go?" Victoria offered.

Harriet looked at Polly, who nodded. "Sure. We can check on Mango."

"You're fond of that little creature, aren't you?" Victoria smiled. "Animals have a way of getting into your heart. Even reptiles."

"Even reptiles," Harriet agreed. "Not that I've worked with many."

They strolled through the zoo, pausing at the monkey cage. "They're so funny," Polly said as the black-and-white colobus monkeys leaped around the trees. "Do they have names?"

"Yes, they do." Victoria named each one, pointing out family groups as well. "*Colobus guereza* are arboreal monkeys from Africa. They rarely come down to the ground, and their mantle and tails act as parachutes when they jump."

"Are they endangered?" Polly asked, sounding worried.

"Not at all," Victoria assured her. "The population is large and healthy."

Polly sighed with relief. She must have found a zoo favorite. Harriet was leaning toward Peanut the elephant, and now she asked if they could go see him.

After gazing adoringly at the elephant while he fed himself, Harriet said, "We're keeping you too long. Is the offer of refreshments still on?"

"Definitely." Victoria gestured. "Follow me." She led them along a side path that was off-limits to guests.

Which was why Harriet was surprised to hear voices a few minutes later.

"This is quite the place you have here." Harriet recognized Ozzie's Australian accent.

"It's not too bad," Nick said. "Quite a lot of acreage still, even if my grandfather sold some to support the zoo."

Victoria stopped dead, putting out a hand to halt Harriet and Polly. She cocked her head, obviously listening hard.

"That must be a costly enterprise," Ozzie mused. "You could always sell off the animals for some ready cash."

Nick laughed. "It hasn't come to that yet."

"But you could, right?" Ozzie pressed. "You could do so much more here. A house that size could be one of those inclusive resorts.

Keep horses, maybe. Toffs really go for those. Hang on to a few of the friendlier animals to provide some color."

Victoria's face flushed a deep red, and her eyes flashed with anger. She started to move forward, but Harriet put a restraining hand on her arm. Although they hadn't tried to eavesdrop, this was an opportunity for Victoria to learn what the men were up to.

"I'm not sure what I can do," Nick said. "As far as I know, the place belongs to Victoria. My father thought I was dead."

"But you aren't." Ozzie's voice sounded sly. "You told me he planned to split everything between you. You definitely have a claim."

"I'll get into it later. Come on. I want to go back to the house."

Silence followed.

Harriet crept around the corner to where the path skirted the rear garden. The grassy area edged with flower beds was empty. "They're gone."

Victoria still hadn't moved, conflicting emotions warring on her face—dismay, sorrow, fear. "I'm happy my brother came back," she said. "Truly I am. But I never imagined it might mean I'd lose the zoo."

"Don't get ahead of yourself," Polly said. "You would still own half, wouldn't you? He would need your agreement before making any changes."

"I think so, yes." Victoria bit her lip. "I need to read the will again. I barely registered anything the attorney said at the reading. I was too upset about losing Dad."

"Why don't you do that?" Harriet said. "Then give the estate lawyer a call. I'm sure they can advise you."

Victoria began moving again. "I will. Soon." She grimaced. "Not that I want to fight with my long-lost brother over money."

"It's not just money," Harriet reminded her. "The zoo animals depend on you. This is their home, as you explained on the tour."

What would happen to the animals if the zoo was to close? She was pretty sure they wouldn't be sent back to their natural environment. Victoria had said many of them didn't have the skills they needed to survive in the wild. It would be up to other zoos to take them in. The problem was that all zoos weren't created equal. How could they guarantee that the animals would continue to receive the excellent care to which they were accustomed?

One step at a time, Harriet reminded herself. They didn't even know what would happen with the property. Why borrow trouble?

"I'm going to stow these in the Beast," she said, indicating her bag and supplies. "Meet you at the house?"

The other two went on, and Harriet cut along a side path toward the parking lot. Her first exotic animal appointment had gone quite well. She'd give Jason an update via text, and hopefully, he would be able to enjoy his time off.

As Harriet closed the Beast's trunk, a police cruiser pulled into the lot. Van. What was he doing here?

"Hey, Harriet," Van called as he climbed out of the car and shut the door. "What brings you here?"

"I was about to ask you the same thing," Harriet said. "We had a call. A zebra with a leg injury." She gestured. "I was about to join Victoria and Polly in the house for a cup of tea."

"Polly?" Van's eyes lit up. "She was assisting you?"

"She was. Did a nice job too, as usual. I had to sedate Zippy, which meant getting out the dart gun."

"Dart gun, huh?" Van eyed her speculatively. "Are you a good shot?"

"Good enough for what I needed to do." Harriet gave a little laugh. "I haven't used one since I moved here."

The discussion of Zippy's cut occupied them all the way to the house. "Come on in," Harriet said, opening the door. As an invited guest, she didn't bother to knock or ring the bell.

Voices drifted their way from the kitchen, so Harriet led Van in that direction. Victoria and Polly were seated at the island, a teapot, milk pitcher, sugar bowl, and several mugs already set out.

Victoria slid off her stool when she saw Van. "DC Worthington. Is there news?"

Van hesitated in the doorway. "There is." He glanced at Harriet and Polly. "We probably should discuss this in private."

Victoria's hands curled into fists. "No. Harriet and Polly are friends. You can tell them anything you would tell me."

Van shifted his stance. "Is your brother here?"

The young woman nodded. "He's around somewhere."

"Why don't you go find him? Then we can talk in the drawing room, if that works for you."

Victoria hurried toward the kitchen door. "I'll do that. Be right back."

Polly pulled off the tea cozy and checked the strength of the brew.

"Is it ready?" Harriet asked. "I'm parched." She had the feeling that another startling revelation lay ahead. If it wasn't important or he was merely checking a detail, Van would have called.

In response, Polly filled three mugs. "Want a cuppa, Van?"

"Love one," he said, crossing the kitchen to the island. She handed him a cup, and he added milk. "Thanks."

"No problem." Polly doctored her own mug after handing Harriet one. "Did Harriet tell you about Zippy?"

Perhaps grateful for a neutral topic, Van's expression lightened. "She did. I wish I'd seen it."

"Poor thing cut his leg. We had to take care of it quick, before he woke up. Fortunately, Harriet knew exactly what to do."

"I had a great helper," Harriet said.

Van didn't let on that Harriet had already told him everything, expressing great interest as Polly relayed the story. They had moved on to the antics of the monkeys when Victoria reappeared.

"Nick is waiting in the drawing room," she said, slightly breathless. "I had to run all over the house to find him." She made a face. "He insisted that Ozzie sit in. So I definitely want Harriet and Polly there." She hesitated. "Unless you're arresting someone."

"Not today, Miss Langford. Just something I need to ask you both about."

The group carried their teacups to the drawing room. There they found Nick pacing in front of the cold fireplace while Ozzie lounged in an armchair, an amused expression on his face.

Harriet wondered whether anything ever bothered Ozzie. Nick, supposedly his good friend, was dealing with a traumatic event, and Ozzie behaved as if he were watching a show.

Van stepped to the middle of the room. They all faced him expectantly, the room so quiet Harriet could hear the distant roar of the lion.

"Good afternoon," Van said. "As you may remember, I'm Detective Constable Van Worthington. The remains of the *Petrel* were recovered and have been moved to dry dock for further examination. I'm here to update you on our recent findings."

Victoria made a small squeak then shook her head when everyone glanced at her. She must have been thinking about her cousin, Scott Spencer.

Van went on. "While examining the sailboat, our team came across an item that we hope you can identify for us, Mr. and Miss Langford." He reached into his pocket and pulled out an evidence bag. He crossed the carpet and held it up so Victoria and Nick could view the contents.

Nick inhaled sharply then coughed as if to hide his reaction.

Victoria reached out a hand, and Van allowed her to take the bag, which contained a tiny carved elephant.

"It's Japanese netsuke," Victoria said. "My grandfather put together quite a collection." She turned to her brother, consternation plain on her face. "What was this doing on the boat?"

CHAPTER NINE

Nick scowled. "How should I know?" he blustered. "It probably came from somewhere else and washed onto the *Petrel*."

Van crossed his arms, his expression skeptical. "We found it inside the cabin," he said. "Near the remains of a zipped canvas bag." He paused. "It wasn't the only piece. They were all bagged in plastic."

Harriet pictured the scene, the cloth rotting after two decades underwater to reveal the bag's contents. Whoever had enclosed the pieces in plastic had meant to protect them from damaging sea water. Which meant they were on board intentionally.

Nick ducked his head, lacing his fingers together.

Victoria took a step toward him. "Did you steal them, Nick? Were you going to sell them to fund your trip?" She shook her head. "Dad would have been devastated if he'd known." Her eyes widened. "Come to think of it, he must have known. He would have noticed missing pieces. They were displayed in his study, in a case."

"We found several," Van repeated. "With all the silt and sand filling the hull, any others might be lost for good."

Victoria lifted her chin. "There's an inventory somewhere. We can check it. But that's the least of my worries right now." Her eyes hadn't left her brother. "Nick, you're going to have to come clean about the shipwreck. And everything else."

He shifted, avoiding her gaze. "What does it matter if I did take them? Which I'm not saying I did. They belong to me." After a pause. "Now."

Van studied the young man for a long moment. "We're merely gathering information, Mr. Langford." He turned to Victoria. "Thank you, Miss Langford. Now that we know you have a collection, we can establish ownership and return the pieces."

"I appreciate that, DC Worthington. If you come with me now, I'll show you the case. I can probably find that inventory list fairly quickly."

"I would appreciate that," Van said. "It would speed things up on our end." He and Victoria left the room.

Harriet was torn. She wanted to leave, to go check on Mango and be on her way, but at the same time, she was curious about what would happen next. She peeked into her cup, which was still half-full. She'd drink the rest, slowly, and then leave.

"Netsuke is nice stuff," Ozzie mused. "Never loses its popularity."

"Animal art is always popular," Polly said. "Harriet's grandfather was a well-known animal painter, and we get lots of visitors at the gallery."

Harriet swallowed a groan. If Nick was a thief, she didn't want to tip him off about valuable art at her grandfather's art studio.

"Is that so?" Ozzie asked. "What was his name?"

"Harold Bailey," Polly said. "I understand you have an export business in arts and crafts. I'd love to see some of them."

Now Harriet understood the method behind Polly's madness. She was discreetly engaging Ozzie to learn more about him and Nick. "So would I," Harriet chimed in.

Beaming, Ozzie pulled out his phone and came over to the sofa where Harriet and Polly were sitting. They scooted apart, and he sat between them so they could both see his screen.

"All handmade by artisans," Ozzie said, swiping through images of carved wooden figures, pots with geometric designs, and colorful baskets. "We find the best work and make sure these talented artists have access to a wider market."

"I love the baskets," Harriet exclaimed. "So many sizes and styles."

Ozzie's expression was cunning. "I can get you a good deal. We'll take it out of our percentage."

Harriet took her phone from her pocket. "Send me the link, and I'll make a decision."

"I want the link too," Polly said. "My mother would love one of those striped baskets."

Ozzie threw Nick a glance. "Already got two new customers. How's that for fast work, Nick?"

His partner was slumped in his chair, staring at his folded hands. He didn't seem to hear Ozzie.

"Here you go, ladies. I've sent the link. Appreciate your business." Ozzie rose to his feet, stretching. "I'm a bit peckish. Let's go grab a bite somewhere, Nick. Any recommendations?" he asked Polly and Harriet.

"You can't go wrong anywhere in the village, but Cliffside Chippy has the best fish and chips around," Polly said.

"That sounds like just the thing," Ozzie said. "Cliffside Chippy it is."

"It's one of my favorite places," Harriet said. In fact, she might go there tonight. She hadn't even thought about dinner. First, though, she was going to check on Mango. She'd also touch base with Victoria and do another walk by Zippy before they left. "I'm going to see our iguana," she told Polly, getting to her feet.

She'd thought Polly might wait around to talk to Van, but her assistant hopped up. "I'll go with you."

"Your iguana?" Ozzie asked.

"Well, not my iguana," Harriet said. "She was a stray. My cousins found her loose on my property, and we brought her here to give her the best possible care." That was all she was going to say. Telling people that Mango was extremely rare and valuable didn't seem like a good idea.

"Interesting," Ozzie said. "Head out in a few, Nick?"

Relieved that Ozzie hadn't asked to see the reptile, Harriet hurried from the room. She would call Officer Crosby tonight and leave a message. The sooner Mango was on her way home, the better.

Polly and Harriet were still watching Mango move about her cage when Victoria entered the conservatory. "Oh good," she said. "You're still here."

"We can't tear ourselves away," Harriet said. "I've never been fond of iguanas, but this one is stealing my heart."

"She is adorable," Polly agreed.

Victoria joined them at the enclosure, watching as the iguana crawled up a branch. "That was interesting," she said. "Finding out that some of the netsuke were missing."

"So you found the list?" Harriet asked.

"I did. Dad kept updated lists of all the art and other valuables in the house in the safe. I was little when the pieces disappeared, so I had no idea. He'd made a line through half a dozen, including an elephant, indicating we didn't have them anymore."

"He never officially reported their disappearance, I'm guessing," Harriet said.

"DC Worthington checked the police files and found no record of it. I'm not surprised. Dad wouldn't report his own son or nephew."

"So he knew they took them?" Harriet asked. "He didn't think someone else did it?" Although the discovery of the elephant pointed toward the boys having taken the pieces, at least onto the boat, she wondered about Marshall's reaction to the theft.

Victoria sighed. "This is all conjecture, you understand, since I can't ask my dad. The netsuke are in a locked case in his study. The key was kept in the safe. Still is."

It would probably be difficult for an outsider to access the key and the display case then. Concluding that Nick or his cousin or both had stolen the netsuke was logical.

"Has your brother said anything?" Harriet asked.

Victoria frowned. "Not a word beyond what you heard." The frown deepened. "I don't know if I can trust my own brother. Isn't that sad, after decades of missing him?"

"Why did Nick leave in the first place?" Harriet asked.

Victoria folded an arm across her middle, tapping her lips with her other hand. "I asked Dad about that a few years ago. He told me Nick and Scott wanted to take a gap year before going to university. He was opposed to that, which led to arguments. I already told you that the night they left, there was a huge blowup. The boys had made plans to sail to Europe and then down to Africa." Her features creased in dismay. "My father blamed himself for the shipwreck. He said if Nick hadn't been so upset, he would have paid more attention to the weather. Dad never got over it."

"I'm so sorry," Harriet said. "What a terrible burden to live with all those years."

Anger sparked in Victoria's eyes. "And to think my brother could have eased his mind by contacting us. He never wrote or called, let alone darkened our door. Dad still would have mourned Scott, of course, but he would have been overjoyed to know Nick survived."

Victoria had a point. Not for the first time, Harriet rued how badly people could hurt each other. Nick was a prodigal son who had returned too late.

Will had a parish meeting, and Polly had made plans with her family, so Harriet ended up going to Cliffside Chippy alone. She didn't mind in the least. The walk along the clifftop gave her a chance to stretch her legs while taking in the rippling ocean and bands of clouds gilded by the sinking sun. She had plenty of time to eat and walk back before dark.

Resolving not to think about troubling topics, Harriet pondered what type of fish she would order. The Chippy offered cod, haddock, and flounder. Maybe she'd get flounder. Its mild sweetness appealed in her current mood.

Catching movement in the low bushes out of the corner of her eye, Harriet jumped. She paused to figure out what it was but couldn't see anything. Probably a chipmunk or a squirrel or even a bird. Laughing at her reaction, she continued on.

Business was relatively slow at the restaurant, with only three or four people ahead of her in line. She was glad to spot some empty tables inside. In milder temperatures, she preferred the picnic tables on the patio, with their view of the harbor and the water beyond, or even on the seawall. But while the early spring weather promised future warmth, it had yet to arrive full force.

As she waited to order the flounder, Harriet recognized the woman standing two spots ahead of her. Ruth Armstrong, from the teashop and the protest rally. According to Victoria, Ruth was also a witness to the sailboat's distress during the storm. Harriet wondered if Ruth had seen Nick yet.

So much for taking a break from pondering the shipwreck and Nick's decades-long disappearance.

Ruth ordered and then moved aside to wait for her food. She caught sight of Harriet and offered her a smile and a nod. Harriet returned the gesture.

After Harriet ordered a small box of flounder plus cups of tea and water, she claimed an empty table with her fleece jacket. Ruth was sitting at the adjacent table, reading a local newspaper while she ate. Harriet almost sat with her back to Ruth but then decided that would be rude, so she draped her jacket over the facing chair.

Ruth raised her head and tapped the newspaper. "Quite an amazing story, isn't it?" The headline referenced the discovery of the *Petrel*.

"It is." Harriet was wary of saying too much in public.

"What a miracle," Ruth went on. "Nick having survived, I mean." She set her jaw. "I saw the boat foundering during the storm."

"That must have been horrible," Harriet said.

"It was." Ruth's expression was bleak. "Nick and Scott were my friends. We used to hang out together as part of the same gang."

"I'm so sorry." Harriet wasn't sure what to say. She hadn't expected Ruth to confide in her. They barely knew each other. Perhaps sometimes it was easier to talk to a stranger.

Harriet's name was called. She excused herself to retrieve her tray then returned to the table, wondering if Ruth would continue talking to her. Harriet had to admit she was curious, mainly about Nick's disappearance. Why hadn't he raised the alarm when he reached the shore? Perhaps Scott could have been saved.

Unless Nick knew for certain that his cousin had drowned. Panic could make people act out of character. So could remorse.

"Mind if I sit with you?" Ruth asked.

What could Harriet say? "Be my guest."

Ruth brought her cup of tea over to Harriet's table and sat across from her, leaving her empty box of fish and chips and the newspaper behind.

"What'd you get?" Ruth asked, peering toward Harriet's dinner.

"The flounder." Harriet doused the fish filet with vinegar and took a savory, mouthwatering bite. "So delicious."

"It is." Ruth let her eat a few bites before continuing. "Do you think I should go see Nick?"

Harriet was taken aback. "I can't answer that. What kind of terms were you on when you last saw him?"

Ruth fiddled with her paper cup. "Not great ones." She was silent for a moment. "I was at the party at Langford Hall the night they left. I knew something was up when I heard shouting in his father's study. Nick was so angry. I'd never seen him like that. A while later, I saw him and Scott leaving the house. They wouldn't say where they were going."

"Right in the middle of the party?" To Harriet, that meant Nick had really been upset and eager to get away from Langford Hall. Surely it would have been more prudent to leave in the morning, even without a storm blowing in.

Ruth shrugged. "The party was winding down. I was still there with a few other people. I followed them outside and asked where Nick was going, but he told me to mind my own business." Her cheeks flushed. "I only asked because I cared. I told him, 'Don't leave like this. You might regret it later.'"

No doubt he had. Nick had never seen his father again.

"They took off in Scott's car. I was worried, so I got in my car and followed them. They headed right to the harbor in White Church Bay, and I caught up with them on the docks."

Harriet had been eating steadily as Ruth spoke, fascinated by her tale. She could picture the scene, the race through the narrow lanes, the confrontation on the waterfront.

"How did they react? I mean, he'd told you not to interfere."

Ruth gave a bitter laugh. "Not well. They were loading bags into the dinghy when I showed up. I begged them not to leave. The clouds were coming in by then, and the wind had started to pick up. But they got into the dinghy and started rowing." She put both hands to her cheeks. Her next words were barely above a whisper. "I told him I hoped he drowned for being so foolish."

"Oh, Ruth." Harriet patted Ruth's arm. "You spoke in anger. I'm sure he knew you didn't mean it." When Ruth didn't respond, she added, "We all say things we regret."

Ruth's gaze dropped to her tea. "I wouldn't blame him if he hasn't forgiven me."

"You didn't cause the sailboat to sink," Harriet reminded her. "The storm did."

Ruth sat silently for a moment then gave a bitter laugh. "What you must think of me, telling you all this out of the blue. You barely know me."

"I have one of those faces, I think," Harriet said, to lighten the moment. "If my patients could talk, they'd all be confiding in me."

Ruth's expression eased into a small smile. "Your animal patients." Her shoulders slumped. "I wish I knew what I should do."

"Why don't you try reaching out to Nick?" Harriet suggested. "Start with something like, 'Hello, I'm glad you're back,' and then see where it goes from there." It seemed to her that Nick had bigger concerns than a decades-old argument with a friend.

Ruth brightened. "Thanks. Maybe I'll do that." She took a sip of tea and wrinkled her nose. "Cold." She sat back in her chair. "Nick never liked the zoo."

"I heard he was bitten by a goat," Harriet said. "Is that why?"

"Partly, maybe. He's not that good with animals." Ruth's smile was reminiscent. "That's not what I mean though. He was opposed to the whole thing. Thought they should disband it." She tapped a finger on the table. "His stance caused a lot of the animosity between him and his father. It wasn't just the gap-year plan. I think his dad said that to save face. Nick probably told him outright that he didn't want to run a zoo. Victoria, obviously, feels the opposite."

"I imagine she's proud to carry on her family's legacy," Harriet reflected. "I know I am."

Ruth heaved a huge sigh. "Makes me wonder what will happen to Moorland Zoo now. If Nick gets his way…"

Harriet silently finished the sentence. *The zoo will close.* She sincerely hoped it didn't come to that, for the sake of Victoria and the animals. But wasn't that what Ruth wanted? She finished her food and wiped her fingers on a napkin. "That was delicious. I love this place."

"Me too." Ruth looked rueful. "I'm sorry I interrupted your meal. Next time, no talk about my problems."

"It's a plan," Harriet said. She had no idea if Ruth's impulsive offer would come to fruition. At least she and the animal activist had established a rapport of sorts. Ruth had said she was searching for a job. With any luck, she'd find one somewhere else and move far away from Moorland Zoo. Victoria didn't need the headache of protestors outside her gates.

Ruth rose to her feet with a stretch. "I guess I'd better get going." She picked up her empty cup and moved to clear her table. "Nice to see you, Harriet."

"You as well." Harriet sat back to drink her own tea and relax before returning to Cobble Hill Farm.

The fish-and-chips shop was almost empty when Harriet took her leave. Bidding a good evening to the servers she'd come to know, she headed out into a pink-and-gold sunset. The sea was still and glassy, holding a reflection of the gorgeous sky. There was almost no wind, and the village lay peacefully in the evening hush.

Her route took her past the church and rectory, and she thought of stopping in for a few minutes, since Will's car was in the drive. Then she remembered her busy roster of appointments in the morning and kept moving. She'd send Will a text once she got home. She would also flip through Grandad's journals for mentions of the Langford family and Moorland Zoo.

On the cliff, she paused to admire the view, the golden light etching every detail of the grass, the tumbling cliff, and the village below.

Low bushes between Harriet and the shore rustled, the sound catching her attention as they had on the way down. This time the cause of the noise came into view.

A dark red snake more than two feet long slithered across the path, passing almost right over the toes of Harriet's sneakers.

CHAPTER TEN

Harriet gasped and jumped back. The snake disappeared into the bushes as she stared after it, stunned. She'd never seen a snake like that in her life. Its tail was blunt, as if it had been chopped off.

A terrible thought gripped Harriet. What if that snake had been smuggled in like Mango?

She pulled her phone out of her jacket pocket and began a search. She typed in the estimated length, color, and the tail's odd shape.

She got a result almost immediately. Comparing the picture to what she'd seen, she believed the snake to be a red sand boa. They weren't rare in their native land of India, but they were heavily trafficked around the world.

Another smuggled reptile had shown up in White Church Bay.

What should she do? It was probably impossible to track the snake, especially as night was falling. But if she didn't try, it might be lost forever. Sand boas needed a warm environment. It might freeze to death if left outside overnight.

Harriet called Van. "Sorry to interrupt your evening, but I've found another imported reptile loose in White Church Bay."

"Another iguana?"

"No," Harriet said. "A snake. I'm up on the cliffside path, and I saw it go into the bushes."

"We do have snakes around here, Harriet."

"I know, but I was able to identify this one. It's from India. It could freeze if we leave it out. I'll send you the picture."

"Oh, boy. If you're right, we'd better try to catch it. I'll be there shortly. Stay where you are."

Keeping an eye on the bushes, Harriet called Will. "Hey," she said when he answered. "Guess where I am?"

"Outside the rectory?" he asked.

"I was, a few minutes ago," she said with a laugh. "Almost stopped in, except I have a busy morning tomorrow. And then I ran into another exotic reptile on the cliff path."

"You're kidding." Will sounded astounded. "Mango has a friend?"

"I'm not sure if they know each other, but this one is a snake. A red sand boa. Van is going to come and try to catch it. It shouldn't be outside on a cold night."

"I'll be right there," Will said. "Where exactly are you?"

Harriet told him, smiling. How lucky was she, with two valiant men rushing to her rescue?

Soon she saw two figures making their way along the path. It was getting dark, and as they drew closer, she saw that Will was holding a large flashlight. Van had a sort of stick resting against one shoulder and carried a burlap sack in his other hand.

"Hello," she called, waving her arms. "Here I am."

"Are you all right?" Will called back.

She laughed. "I'm perfectly fine. I was a little spooked when the snake burst out of the bushes and almost went over my shoes."

"That would startle anyone," Van said, lowering the stick.

"What is that?" Harriet asked.

"Professional snake-catching tongs," Van said. "I got them at an animal-control seminar. Our dog catcher has been overwhelmed with calls lately, so some of us on the force have taken courses to help lighten his load. Never thought I'd actually use these though."

"What's the plan?" Will asked.

Van glanced around the area. "Where did you see it go, Harriet?"

She pointed out the route the snake had taken, into an area of grass and wildflowers mixed with bilberry and cotoneaster shrubs. "Hopefully it didn't go too far."

"I bet it's hiding under a bush," Will said. "That's what I'd do."

Van traced a straight line to the closest thick bush. He readied the tongs and the stick. "Get ready to shine the light, Will. Go."

As the light's bright beam shone on the undergrowth, Van pushed branches aside with his tongs. Something moved, the grass parting.

"Got you." Van lifted the snake with the tongs, lowered it into the open sack, and then closed it quickly.

Harriet clapped. "That was great, Van. Your instructor would be proud."

Van puffed out his chest. "Got lucky, didn't I? Can we take our new friend to your clinic, for tonight at least? I'll give Officer Crosby a call in the morning."

"Absolutely." Harriet had several cages available that would work.

Eager to safely contain the stray snake, the trio walked the rest of the way at a brisk pace. Harriet was grateful for Will's bright light, which he used to illuminate tricky areas. They didn't need to add a fall to the evening's adventures.

Back at the clinic, Harriet unlocked the door and led the way inside, where they chose a cage for the snake. Harriet held the door while Van gently freed the snake from the sack inside the cage then shut the door before it could try to escape.

"I'd better get a water dish at least," Harriet said. "I don't have anything suitable for it to eat."

"What's their diet?" Will asked.

"Small rodents," Harriet said, recalling what she'd read while waiting for Van and Will to join her on the path. "I don't have any of those handy."

Will shuddered. "Count me out at feeding time."

"I hear you," Harriet said. "But boas can go days or weeks without eating. I hope we can find another home for it with someone who knows more than I do and can tell when it's hungry." She couldn't see herself keeping the snake long-term. Maybe Victoria would want it. Moorland Zoo had a few snakes.

After turning on a self-regulated warming light, Harriet asked, "Cup of tea, anyone? I need to unwind after all this excitement."

"I'll take one, thanks." Van snapped some pictures of the snake with his phone. "For my report. And to send to the wildlife authorities."

As they made their way to the kitchen, Will mused, "I wonder if the snake and Mango were brought in by the same smuggler."

"Let's hope so." Harriet switched on the kitchen light, and Maxwell came running. "Look, Maxwell," Harriet said. "Here's some friends come to see you." Maxwell wiggled all over as the two men fussed over him. "That's all we need," Harriet went on. "White Church Bay becoming a smuggling hub."

Van's smile was rueful. "As it was in the past? We're not that far from Europe as the crow flies, remember."

"Maybe the reptiles came from the German show that was held recently," Harriet suggested as she filled the kettle. "I was reading about it online. There's a similar event in York soon."

Van leaned his tongs against the wall and took a seat at the kitchen table. "It's possible they came from Germany. I'll ask Crosby about that. Whoever had them sure was careless. How many other exotic reptiles are roaming around the countryside as we speak?"

"None, I hope. Or at least none who won't survive our nontropical weather," Will said. He moved easily around the kitchen as he helped Harriet set the table for tea. "Although we probably should alert the local residents to be on the lookout."

"Tough call," Van said. "That might cause a panic. We've been lucky that Harriet was able to intervene both times. Someone else might have thought they were pests."

Harriet leaned against the counter, waiting for the water to boil. It was a puzzle how and why the creatures had gotten loose. Mango was valuable. Harriet doubted someone would have deliberately freed her.

Will gestured to a tin holding lemon curd tarts from Doreen. "Okay if we eat these?"

"Please. Otherwise, I will." Harriet adored lemon curd.

The kettle whistled, and Harriet filled three mugs. Will helped ferry the tea. Van helped himself to a lemon tart.

Harriet regarded her friends with gratitude. How fortunate she was to have two such intrepid men to call upon in an emergency. "Slippery can't say it, so I will. Thanks for your help tonight."

"Slippery?" Will's brow creased. "That's quite a name."

Van chuckled as he thumbed his chest. "He or she wasn't slippery enough to evade DC Worthington."

"No one is," Will said. "Between you, Harriet, and Polly, it's a wonder anyone dares to break the law in White Church Bay."

"I wish that were so," Van murmured, all traces of humor gone.

After Will and Van left, Harriet headed for the study to search through her grandfather's journals. They spanned years, from when he was a young vet student until the end of his life. Almost daily he had recorded interesting or unusual cases, observations, and important local news. Although Harriet wished more than anything that she had Old Doc Bailey to consult in person, the journals were a substitute of sorts.

The sailboat had sunk twenty years before. Harriet wasn't sure of the exact date, so she consulted news articles on her phone before starting her search. Once she had the right month, she pulled out several journals, taking the year before and after for good measure. She hoped to find entries about the zoo animals as well, figuring she needed to learn as much as possible.

A zebra today. Who knew what she'd get for a call tomorrow?

Harriet deposited the journals on the table in her reading nook, an alcove in the living room furnished with a comfortable chair and an ottoman for Charlie. At night, especially when it was cold, Harriet drew the long curtains behind the chair to create a cozy retreat.

Finally, she went into the kitchen for another cup of tea and a tart. The men had greatly reduced the number of tarts, which meant less temptation for her.

After removing Maxwell's wheels and settling him beside her in the chair, Harriet leafed through the journal to the date of the sailboat accident and discovered that a few days before the sinking, Grandad had answered a vet call at the zoo.

> *Made a call at Moorland Zoo to treat a lion's injured paw. Helen would have been nervous about it, God rest her soul, even after I reassured her he'd be sedated.*

Helen was Harriet's late grandmother.

> *In fact, Marshall Langford did the honors. He's qualified to sedate the animals, which is obviously important in case a professional like me isn't available.*
>
> *After we treated the lion—Marshall acting as my assistant—I stayed for tea. We had a nice chat about the zoo and its future. Marshall is worried. His son has no interest in keeping it going. In fact, he's challenging Marshall about the ethics of zoos in general. Marshall chalks this up to the influence of a certain young lady.*

Could he be talking about Ruth? That would fit with her present activism.

> *He's hoping that university will help Nick mature and take a broader view. All I could offer was empathy and my own experience. To Helen's credit, our children's transition to adulthood was fairly smooth. Not everyone can be so*

lucky. I pray that Nick's current attitude is a phase he'll grow out of.

The entry ended there, and Harriet paused to drink some tea and welcome Charlie, who strolled into the room and curled up on the ottoman. How poignant and sad, considering the rest of the story. She'd also learned something new. If her assumption was correct, that Ruth had been influencing Nick even then, perhaps it hadn't been a good idea to urge her to contact him. Harriet would feel awful if Ruth made life more difficult for Victoria.

Harriet turned the pages until she found the entry about the shipwreck.

Something dreadful has happened, leaving a pall of sorrow over White Church Bay. Two young men, Nick Langford and Scott Spencer, lost their lives when their small sailboat went down in a storm.

A witness saw the boat struggling in a sudden squall, but no one has been able to locate it. The Petrel *has sadly joined the many ships lost off the Yorkshire coast.*

Jinny and I are going over later to provide as much comfort as we can. One thing I'm certain of is that the community will rally around this family. The Langfords have been generous donors and good stewards of their property, with the zoo bringing much joy to generations of youngsters.

Harriet took another break to absorb the entry. She cradled her mug in both hands, caught by her grandfather's simple yet evocative words. What a terrible and sad story. Again, she had the advantage of hindsight. She knew Nick had survived. But instead of going home to reassure his family, he'd taken off.

Harriet wondered again, what exactly happened on the sailboat that night?

Only one person knew for sure, and he wasn't talking.

CHAPTER ELEVEN

"Hello? Harriet, are you here?" Polly's footsteps tapped through the clinic.

"Come see our new guest," Harriet called from the back room, where she was checking on Slippery. To her relief, the snake seemed to have survived the night in fine form.

"What guest?" Polly stepped into the room then recoiled when she saw the snake. "Where did that come from?"

"It's a long story." Harriet checked the clock. "We have time to chat before the first appointment. They called to push it back fifteen minutes."

Polly rolled up her sleeves. "Perfect. Can I make you some coffee?"

"I can do it." Harriet led the way to the kitchen, where Polly put the kettle on for her own tea.

Harriet mentally reviewed her schedule while she made coffee. She wanted to call Officer Crosby, both about Slippery and for an update on Mango's upcoming return to the Bahamas. Although Van had said he would get in touch with the officer, Harriet figured it wouldn't hurt if she did too. Sometimes a squeaky wheel did get the grease. And when it came to animal welfare, Harriet was more than willing to squeak.

She poured herself a cup of coffee then turned around to find Polly giving Charlie and Maxwell treats.

"They have you well trained," Harriet said with a laugh.

Polly put the treat containers back. "It's part of their compensation package as the clinic animals."

Harriet laughed as she took a tart, leaving the last one for Polly. "I hope Doreen brings us these again. Although they're deadly for my waistline."

Polly sat at the table, mug of tea in hand. "Hardly, with how active you are."

Harriet considered her point. "I guess I am." She did spend a lot of time outside, tromping over hill and dale to care for cattle, sheep, and horses.

"So how'd we wind up with a snake?" Polly asked.

After a brief description of her dinner at Cliffside Chippy and her encounter with Ruth, Harriet got into the meat of the story. "And there I was, on the cliff path at sunset, alone with a snake."

"Were you worried it would bite you? Or follow you home?" Polly's forehead was creased with confusion. "I don't understand. Why didn't you run away?"

"Because I researched it, and it's definitely not a native species. I called Van and Will." At the mention of Van, Polly's face brightened. Harriet decided to talk him up. "Van was my hero. He's been trained in snake handling, and he had the right equipment."

"You can't be serious," Polly exclaimed. "What do you mean, he's trained?"

"He's taken animal-control courses recently." Harriet took a sip then relayed the sand boa's dramatic capture. "I call Slippery 'it' because I don't know if it's a boy or girl."

"Van wasn't afraid of getting bitten?" Polly asked.

"Not that I could tell. He handled it all calmly. I was quite impressed."

"How about Will?" Polly asked. "Was he worried?"

"He jumped right in to help. Not a nerve in sight."

Polly rested her chin on her hand with a sigh. "I wish I'd been there. I missed all the excitement."

"I'm sure there will be more." Harriet took a deep breath, wanting to broach a certain subject but afraid she was overstepping. "Things went well with Van on the boat ride."

Polly tilted her head. "They did. I was a little taken aback when I saw him, but it turned out okay. We actually talked last night. Via text."

"Oh?" Harriet asked, hoping Polly would elaborate.

"We both decided we're okay being friends, remember? Which means that if we see each other in public or even hang out with you guys, it'll be fine. The boat was a good practice run for that kind of thing."

"That's great." Harriet thought she saw more than friendship, but she wasn't going to say anything. If Van and Polly were meant to be together, it would happen. Meanwhile, she and Will could feel less guarded when the pair encountered each other.

Setting the delicate topic aside, Harriet glanced at the time. "I'm going to give Officer Crosby a call before we start work. I want to check on Mango's status and tell him about the boa."

"Do you think the two incidents are related?" Polly asked. "I think it's strange we found two exotic reptiles within days of each other."

Harriet drank the rest of her coffee. "So do I. Hopefully, he'll figure it out before more reptiles are smuggled in." Maybe there was a weak spot in the border defenses. If so, it would be better to find it sooner rather than later.

Polly went into the clinic to unlock the door and boot up the computer while Harriet ducked into the study to make the call. Officer Crosby's direct line went to voice mail, so she left a message. Then she looked up the closest border control station and called there, where she learned that he was out in the field. She left a message anyway, hoping he might check in.

A dog barked out in the clinic. That was her cue. Time to get to work.

"Did Officer Crosby call?" Harriet asked Polly around midmorning. She'd been bouncing from one patient to the next, so Polly would have taken a message.

"Not yet," Polly said. "Maybe he's out of range."

Harriet clenched her teeth in frustration. "I'm worried about Slippery. I really don't know much about taking care of snakes." She also didn't want the task of procuring the kind of food Slippery needed.

"Do you think the zoo will take it?" Polly asked. "They have snakes."

Harriet flipped through folders for the upcoming appointments. "I had that thought as well. I hesitate to ask Victoria directly, in case there's another protocol I should follow."

"You could call Jason," Polly suggested.

"I don't want to disturb him on vacation if I can help it."

"How about one of the other exotic vets then?" Polly suggested. "Didn't he give you a couple of names?"

"He sure did." Harriet stacked the folders neatly. "In fact, he sent their numbers to my phone." She'd left her phone in the back, on a counter out of the way.

After a quick peek at Slippery, who was basking in the warmth of the artificial light, Harriet scooped up her phone, found Jason's list, and dialed. "Slippery, you're going to be fine, I promise. Hang in there."

The vet, Sherry Fowler, picked up, and Harriet laid out the situation.

"I'd take the snake to a zoo if you're not set up for care," advised the young woman. "That species isn't rare, so I doubt it will be returned to its country of origin."

"We also found an endangered rock iguana," Harriet said. "She'll be sent back."

"Oh, I heard about that," Sherry said. "So fortunate that you found her. They're tropical creatures, so she wouldn't do well in this climate."

"She's at Moorland Zoo while we wait for her departure," Harriet said. "Thanks for your help. I'll take the snake there too, if they want it."

"If not, give me a call," Sherry said. "We'll find a home for it. Don't you worry."

"Thank you." Harriet hung up, relieved that the vet community was providing such support. She'd call Victoria right now and see if she could drop Slippery off after hours.

When closing time rolled around, Harriet still hadn't heard from Officer Crosby. In this case, maybe no news wasn't good news. As in, Mango's travel arrangements still hadn't been made.

"Want to take a ride with me out to the zoo?" Harriet asked Polly, who was entering patient information into the computer. "I'm taking the snake there. Victoria said she had room—and plenty of food."

"I won't ask for details," Polly said with a laugh. "Sure, I'll go. Let me finish up this data entry."

Footsteps sounded in the back, followed by a familiar voice calling, "Hello? Harriet?" Aunt Jinny. She must have checked the house first and then entered the clinic through the rear door. Harriet did the same when she went next door to visit her aunt. They didn't stand on ceremony.

"We're up front," Harriet called.

Aunt Jinny gave a shout.

Harriet and Polly exchanged a smile. "Slippery," Harriet said.

Aunt Jinny entered the front room, mouth agape and one hand on her chest. "That snake startled me. I was expecting to see a cute little dog or cat."

"Slippery is another stray," Harriet said. "Discovered last night on the cliff path."

"What?" Aunt Jinny squawked. "Do you think there are more?"

Harriet sighed. "I hope not. We're taking Slippery over to the zoo in a few minutes. Come talk to me while I get ready."

Her aunt followed Harriet to the back room. "I wanted to invite you over for dinner. I'm making a chicken shepherd's pie."

"That sounds delicious." Harriet studied Slippery's cage. She could transport the snake in that, thankfully. The idea of transferring the reptile to another enclosure was daunting. She gestured. "Can you grab one end?"

Aunt Jinny eyed the cage dubiously. "I guess so."

"Polly," Harriet called as they carried the cage in tandem, "open the back of the Beast, will you please?"

Polly hurried outside to the Land Rover and opened it so Harriet and Aunt Jinny could slide the cage inside. That task complete, Harriet told her aunt about the adventures of the previous evening. "It was lucky for the snake that I happened by," she concluded. "Otherwise, it might have suffered from hypothermia."

"Who is doing this?" Aunt Jinny demanded. "It's terribly irresponsible."

"I agree." Harriet couldn't resist teasing her. "Keep your eyes open when you're outside. There might be more escapees lurking."

Aunt Jinny shuddered. "Please don't say that. Snakes can get in practically anywhere, you know. The smallest crack or hole in a foundation."

"Well, give me a call if you see one," Harriet said. "Or, actually, why don't you call Van? He's the expert handler."

"I'll put him on speed dial," Aunt Jinny said with a chuckle. "See you around six? Polly, you're welcome to eat with us."

"Thank you." Polly beamed with pleasure. "I'd be happy to join you."

Aunt Jinny returned home, and Harriet and Polly gathered their handbags and locked up the clinic and house. Then they set off for the zoo.

Victoria was waiting for them in the parking lot, standing beside a golf cart. She waved as they pulled into a space beside hers.

"I didn't know you had a golf cart," Harriet said as she climbed out of the Land Rover. That would have saved them a hike the day they'd treated Zippy the zebra.

"It needed repair when you were here before," Victoria said. "Nick fixed it. He's quite talented when it comes to engines of all sorts."

"That's handy." Harriet opened the back of the Beast. "Want to bring it a little closer?"

Victoria did so then came over to look at the snake. "A red sand boa. So cool."

"I read they're a popular breed to traffic," Harriet said. "Apparently, they're docile and not venomous." Thankfully, she hadn't found an asp or a cobra. Those could be dangerous.

"We'll take good care of him? Her?" Victoria asked.

"I didn't check," Harriet said. "Not my area of expertise."

"We can do it." Victoria gestured at the cage. "Need help?"

"We've got it." Harriet and Polly each picked up an end and placed the cage in the cart's cargo area. Then they hopped aboard for the short ride to the reptile house.

They pulled up in front of the structure, which featured indoor and outdoor areas for the reptiles. "This enclosure is heated,"

Victoria explained. "Most of the reptiles are from warm climates, so we keep them cozy."

Harriet and Polly again hefted the cage and carried it inside at Victoria's instruction. At one end, an enclosure sat with its door open. It was full of decorative touches that Harriet assumed were reminiscent of the boa's natural environment. "This cage is the right size," Victoria said.

Now that they were there, Harriet wondered what their next step was.

She needn't have worried. With an air of competent confidence, Victoria put on a pair of gloves and picked up tongs like Van's. With several deft movements, she had Slippery out of the travel cage and into the enclosure. She shut the door and studied the snake, who began moving around, exploring. "Ah, someone's hungry. See the tongue movements? Don't worry, buddy, we'll get you sorted in no time."

"I'm glad you're set up for that," Harriet said.

"No problem." Still watching the snake, Victoria smiled. "I've been handling reptiles since I was a toddler. Always freaks boys out when I mention it, for some reason."

Polly laughed. "The right guy will recognize how amazing you are."

Victoria gave a little shrug, her cheeks flushing. "About that…"

"You've met someone?" Harriet was glad. Now that she was happy with Will, she enjoyed seeing friends couple up happily. Or in Polly's case, make movements in that direction. Maybe if Van did a little lion taming next…

"I think so," Victoria said. "He's awfully nice. We're going to get together next week when he gets back from vacation."

Two and two easily led to four. "Jason Peel, right?" Harriet guessed.

Victoria nodded with a smile. "It's early days yet, of course, but we certainly have a lot in common. Mainly a passion for animals. He's not afraid of snakes either."

Harriet guessed he wouldn't be, as an exotic animal vet. They dealt with all kinds of rare and dangerous creatures.

Victoria went to the food supply room and soon returned with a meal for Slippery. "We'll leave him to eat in peace," she said as she shut the cage. "Do you have time to come up to the house?"

Harriet checked her phone. They had a good hour before dinner at Aunt Jinny's. "We can do that."

Once again, they climbed aboard the golf cart. Victoria took a different route, driving them past Zippy's enclosure. The zebra was grazing, moving around without any issues.

"You did a great job with him," Victoria said. "I'm really pleased."

"So am I," Harriet said. "Not bad for my first zebra case."

As they drove out of the zoo gate, Harriet noticed a white van with blue and black checks parked in the lot. Border Force. "Officer Crosby has finally surfaced. Maybe there's news about Mango."

"Let's go find out." Victoria drove the cart along the wide garden path to the rear entrance.

As they approached the back door, it opened. Nick came out first, holding the door, and then Officer Crosby emerged. The Border Force agent carried a small cage.

Mango was inside.

CHAPTER TWELVE

Victoria hurried to intercept the agent. "I didn't know you were coming. Why didn't you call?"

Officer Crosby made as though to brush her aside. "Someone from the agency was supposed to let you know."

Victoria checked her phone. "I don't see a call."

The Border Force agent shrugged. "They're pretty busy. Must have been an oversight. I assure you that I have orders to take the iguana. Please let me pass."

"Did the Wildlife Crimes Unit arrange transport?" Harriet asked. She kept pace with Officer Crosby, who was still walking. "Goodbye, Mango. Have a nice trip home. Hope you find your family."

The officer regarded her with skepticism. "It's an iguana."

"They have families too." Harriet bit back any further argument, knowing she had to stay on good terms with the Border Force. She might be dealing with Officer Crosby on a regular basis, although she hoped not.

Still walking beside him, she asked, "Did you get my message? We found a smuggled sand boa. It's in the reptile house here."

He spared her a brief glance. "Could be an escaped pet. Sand boas are common, even if not legal. We don't do much about them. They're not endangered."

Effectively rebuffed, Harriet stopped walking. "Okay. Thanks for the information." She raised her voice. "Bye, Mango."

Harriet walked back to her friends. "That's that, I guess. Mango is flying home."

Victoria patted her arm. "I know how you feel. I get attached every single time." She gestured toward the house. "Can you stay for a few minutes?"

Harriet glanced at Polly, who nodded. "Sure. We're not in a hurry."

Nick had disappeared back inside the house, and Harriet didn't see him when they walked through to the kitchen. She wondered how it was going between the siblings, but she didn't want to pry.

Harriet and Polly sat at the counter while Victoria remained standing, leaning against the island. "This is getting to be a regular thing, you coming out here," she said. "I like it."

"We do too," Harriet said. "Certainly is a break in the routine."

Polly swiveled her tall chair. "That's what you wanted, isn't it?" she asked Harriet.

"Yes," Harriet said. She turned to Victoria. "I've been trying to fend off a bad case of spring fever," she explained.

"We need to plan another activity," Polly said. "Something not work related."

Harriet was glad Polly hadn't talked about the boat tour, Harriet's first effort to change up her routine. A mention of the sunken sailboat would likely dredge up painful memories for Victoria.

"Any ideas?" Harriet asked. She'd been so busy lately, she'd focused strictly on the day-to-day.

"How about a ramble on the moors?" Polly suggested. "They're gorgeous in the spring."

"I second that idea," Victoria said. "But don't go out when it's misty. There are old mine workings and cliffs to fall over."

"Not to mention the bogs," Polly agreed. "If you wander in, you'll be up to your knees in cold, wet muck."

Harriet chuckled. "Great sales pitch. Maybe we should skip it." She didn't want to risk her life going for a walk. That would be a little too much excitement.

"No worries," Polly said. "We'll pick a sunny, clear day. Make sure we have a map and compass and the right clothing."

"All right, I'll give it a try," Harriet said.

Victoria glanced at the wall clock. "I suppose I should go clean out Mango's cage."

Harriet and Polly trailed out to the conservatory behind Victoria. Their hostess went over to the now-empty cage. She opened the door. "Not too bad. A quick wipe-down will sort it out."

Harriet watched the genets moving around in their cage while Victoria fetched cleaning supplies. They really were cute, like a cross between cats and weasels. Then she noticed something. "How many genets do you see?" she asked Polly.

"Are we playing a game?" Polly asked, amused. "The twins told me about Spot the Genet."

"Not exactly," Harriet said, trying to push down a feeling of foreboding.

Polly studied the cage for a moment. "Three. They're not easy to count, the way they duck behind things and hide."

"Three? Are you sure?" Harriet was positive Victoria had told the twins there were four.

Victoria entered the room, carrying a tote filled with cleaning supplies. "Aren't the genets adorable? I think they're getting less shy now that they see people every day."

"How many did you say you have?" Harriet asked, trying to sound casual and unconcerned.

Victoria bent and set the tote on the floor near Mango's cage. "Four. Two pairs. We're hoping for babies at some point."

"Um, I can only see three," Harriet said.

Polly had come to stand beside her, and she chimed in, "That's all I see too."

"What?" Victoria straightened. "That can't be." She peered into the cage, her gaze flicking around the interior. "No! One is missing." She sounded frantic. "There's no way. I never leave the cage open." She dashed across the large room to the doorway. "Nick," she called. "Where are you?"

"Maybe Officer Crosby took it," Polly said.

"I don't see why," Harriet objected. "They belong to the zoo."

Polly shook her head. "There's something about him I don't like."

Harriet had to admit she agreed with Polly. She tried to reserve judgment, however. First impressions weren't always correct.

Victoria returned a couple minutes later. "I can't find either of the guys. They must have gone somewhere." She went to stand in front of the cage, searching again, as if she might find the spotted creature this time.

"Could the genet have gotten out somehow?" Harriet asked.

"I don't think so." Victoria checked the cage doors. "They're latched good and tight." She reached into her back pocket and took out a phone. "I'm going to text Nick. Maybe they let one out by accident and didn't want to tell me."

That seemed a likely scenario to Harriet. The genets were adorable little animals and quite inquisitive.

Victoria slid the phone back into her pocket. "Hopefully, they know what happened."

Harriet and Polly watched while Victoria pulled on rubber gloves and started cleaning the empty cage.

Something pinged, and Victoria stopped working. She tugged off her gloves to check her phone. "Nick said he has no idea what happened to the genet. Neither does Ozzie."

As Victoria started to put her phone back, Harriet said, "Maybe you should report it missing? If the genet did get out somehow, someone might find it."

Victoria nodded. "You're right. I wouldn't want them to think it's a weasel after their chickens or whatever." She stood with fingers poised. "Who should I call?"

"I'd try DC Worthington," Harriet said. "He'll make sure the word gets out."

"Good idea." Victoria began scrolling. "He seems like a really good guy."

Harriet grinned. "He is. Exotic animal rescue is becoming a bigger part of his job than he expected."

Victoria laughed. "Seems like it lately." She put the phone to her ear. "DC Worthington? It's Victoria Langford. I've got another case for you."

After she hung up, she said, "He'll be out here shortly to take a statement. As you suggested, Harriet, he's going to put out a bulletin locally." She put the phone down and picked up her rubber gloves.

"Great." Harriet stretched. "I suppose we'd better get back."

Victoria's phone rang, and she answered. After a moment she said, "A detective inspector from county headquarters? About the genet?" Victoria's tone rose in surprise. Then it sank, along with her expression. "Oh. About the shipwreck. Yes, I'll be here. Thank you, Detective Constable. See you soon."

"What is it?" Harriet asked.

Victoria looked unsettled. "They're coming to talk to me—to us—about the shipwreck. DC Worthington said there's news." She swallowed. "It must be about Scott. Maybe they've identified him. I mean, we know it's him. It's just…"

Harriet hugged her friend. "I'm so sorry."

Polly joined the hug. "It's like losing him all over again, isn't it?"

"Exactly." Victoria dashed tears from her cheeks. "I'll be glad we can put him to rest after so long."

Harriet glanced at the time. They really should go, but she didn't want to leave Victoria alone. "I'm going to give Aunt Jinny a call. We're going to be late for dinner."

"No, I'm okay, you don't have to—" Victoria protested.

"We know we don't have to," Polly cut in gently. "We want to. Besides, Aunt Jinny would have our heads if we didn't stay and support you. Isn't that right, Harriet?"

"Without a doubt." Harriet made the call. After she hung up, she said, "Dinner will be kept warm, so we can eat whenever."

"She's the best," Polly said. "I knew she'd understand."

Victoria was on the phone. "You need to get back here now, Nick.... I don't care.... Tell them to pack it up to go.... A DI from the county will be here shortly.... No, not about the genet.... Right, that's what I think too. See you soon." She hung up.

Harriet and Polly exchanged a questioning glance.

Victoria started to pull on her gloves again but then tossed them aside. "This can wait."

They all trailed into the kitchen, where Victoria began to scrub at the already clean counters. Harriet could sympathize with her restlessness. No matter what the police had to say, it was going to be bad news.

Footsteps and male voices sounded in the back corridor, and Harriet guessed that Nick and Ozzie had returned. The police would have rung the bell or knocked.

Nick sauntered into the kitchen, his gaze roaming over Harriet and Polly. "Hey. How are you?"

"We're fine, thanks," Harriet said.

"I asked them to stay," his sister said. "Ozzie is your support. They're mine."

Ozzie clapped a hand on Nick's shoulder. "Always here for you, mate. You know that."

Nick shrugged his friend's hand off. "I'm not being supportive?" he demanded of his sister.

She ducked her head, polishing a gleaming section of counter. "Of course you are, Nick. It's just that...well, we're getting to know each other again, that's all."

Victoria had been five when Nick went missing, so it made sense that they needed to rebuild their relationship. She wasn't a child anymore, and they needed to meet on an adult footing. Despite this logic, Harriet sensed there was more—that Victoria didn't really trust her brother. Was it because of the zoo and how he might try to claim ownership? Or was it something else?

With a scowl, Nick took a seat at the island.

"Any luck finding a location for your business?" Victoria asked.

The two men exchanged glances. Ozzie, who had been standing, sat beside Nick. "I've been thinking," Nick said. "There's plenty of room here for an office. And we can repurpose an outbuilding for a warehouse."

"I thought you wanted to be closer to the city," Victoria said. "For the traffic."

"Maybe at some point," Nick said. "Renting a warehouse isn't cheap. I figure we can mail orders to retail outlets. Or even deliver, if they're close enough."

Victoria pressed her lips together. "It sounds like a reasonable plan. Let's talk about it later, shall we, Nick?" Her gaze flicked to Ozzie briefly before returning to her brother.

Nick nodded. "Sure. We can do that."

Harriet caught Ozzie scowling, but when he met her eye, his expression changed. "You must be glad old Mango is on her way home," he said. "Quite a responsibility taking care of such a valuable creature."

"It is," Harriet said. "But I also treat racehorses and pedigreed dogs. So high-value animals aren't exactly rare in my world."

Polly hid a grin behind her hand. Standing where only Harriet could see, she gave her a thumbs-up.

Seeming to shrug off her words, Ozzie began to hum and tap his fingers on the counter. But Harriet noticed telltale red creeping up his neck and the glare he covertly sent her way. Ozzie was one to watch out for. He wasn't as easygoing and good-natured as he pretended to be.

As the moments crawled by, Harriet felt uneasy—as did Victoria, judging by the way she paced to and from the windows, peering outside every few seconds. What new bombshell would drop today?

Ozzie's exclamation broke the silence. "I'm not needed here, am I, mate? I think I'll take a little stroll around the grounds."

So much for his expression of support, Harriet thought.

Nick shrugged. "Suit yourself."

"Please don't bother the animals," Victoria said sharply. "Actually, I'd prefer it if you didn't go into the zoo."

Ozzie threw up both hands. "Yes ma'am. I'll keep my distance—don't you worry." With a chuckle and a clap on Nick's shoulder, he left the kitchen. A moment later, the back door slammed shut.

"Why did you bring him here?" Victoria asked her brother. "I don't like him."

Nick's expression was bewildered. "He's my business partner, Vic. What else was I supposed to do?"

A furrow creased her brow. "I don't know. Have him get his own place, maybe?"

"Why?" Nick waved a hand. "We've got this giant house and all these empty bedrooms." He leaned forward, lowering his voice. "I have to stay on good terms with him. He owns most of the company. I'll lose my investment if we end the partnership now."

Arms folded, Victoria mulled that over. "Why don't we talk about this later, in more detail? We'll figure something out."

Relief flashed in Nick's eyes. "Thanks." He gave her a wan smile. "I'm so sorry. You—"

The front doorbell rang.

"I'll get that." Victoria bustled out of the room.

Harriet recognized the officers who came into the room with Van. Detective Inspector Kerry McCormick and Sergeant Adam Oduba.

DI McCormick's gaze went directly to Harriet and Polly. "We meet again."

"Hello," Harriet said. She wondered if the district inspector would ask them to leave.

As if sensing that possibility, Victoria chimed in, "I want them to stay. They've been with me throughout this ordeal, as DC Worthington knows."

DI McCormick nodded. "All right."

Van made introductions, and the Langford siblings murmured the usual "Nice to meet you."

"I'm sorry for your loss," the DI told them. "We have positive identification on the remains found aboard the *Petrel*."

"Scott," Victoria said in a choked voice. "I knew it, but it's still awful." Her shoulders began to shake, and Harriet slipped off her stool and put an arm around her.

Nick sat staring into space, his face blank. Of course, this wasn't a shock to him. He had been aboard the sailboat.

"Unfortunately, that's correct. And there's more," DI McCormick said.

Victoria lifted her head, staring at the officer with red-rimmed eyes. "What more could there be?" Her hands curled into fists. "How can this get any worse?"

The inspector took a deep breath, as if bracing herself. In her acquaintance with the woman, Harriet had come to know her as a brisk, no-nonsense type. She couldn't remember a single time the DI had had to brace herself for anything.

Yet even with that warning, Harriet wasn't prepared for what the inspector said next. "The coroner found an injury to the skull that requires further investigation. Nicholas Langford, we'd like you to come down to the station for questioning."

CHAPTER THIRTEEN

Harriet felt her mouth drop open. That meant the police didn't believe the injury could be explained by the shipwreck itself. Cold dread gripped her. Had Nick caused Scott's death? Maybe that was why he had run away.

Victoria's spine straightened. "Surely you're not saying—Nick?"

"We've haven't come to any conclusions yet," the inspector told her. "Mr. Langford, are you willing to come with us, or should we escalate the matter?" Sergeant Oduba took one step toward Nicholas to emphasize that they meant business.

Nick, still horribly blank-faced, slid off his seat. "I'll go. Vic, maybe give our attorney a call? If we still have one."

"We do," Victoria said, her voice wooden. "Same firm, but his daughter has taken over. I'll go do that now."

Harriet hurried to intercept Victoria on her way out of the room. How could she leave her to deal with this alone? "After you call, would you like to come home with me? My aunt is making dinner. I'll bring you back later." Aunt Jinny wouldn't mind setting another place. Maybe a dose of her maternal care would help Victoria as well.

Victoria hesitated then said, "That would be nice. Thank you." Her smile was wan. "Not that I'll eat much, but I'll appreciate the company."

"That's what I thought." Harriet let her continue on.

Meanwhile, the police officers were escorting Nick out through the front hall. He wasn't cuffed, which meant this wasn't an official arrest. Yet.

"What's the plan?" Polly asked when they were alone in the kitchen.

"I'm not sure," Harriet confessed. "I have to tell you, I'm in shock."

"Me too." Polly tapped her fingers on the counter. "Maybe they fought over those figurines."

"It's possible." Harriet forced disturbing images out of her mind. "I'd rather not speculate."

"No, we shouldn't," Polly agreed. "The police will figure it out." After a pause, she said, "Van is stepping up his game, isn't he? The first time we met DI McCormick, she definitely regarded him as just the local bobby. Now she seems to respect him."

"As she should," Harriet said briskly. "He's doing a fantastic job. Not to mention keeping us safe from snakes."

Polly grinned while Harriet sent a quick text to her aunt about the change in plans. As she'd expected, her aunt was fine with an impromptu guest.

Victoria strode into the kitchen. "Our attorney is meeting Nick at the station. That's one load off my mind."

Harriet patted her shoulder. "I'm glad Nick has someone in his corner. We're ready when you are."

Victoria located her handbag. "I'm all set." She frowned. "I wonder where Ozzie went. He doesn't have a key, as far as I know."

"Did he leave?" Harriet asked. "You'd think he would have come to find out what the police were doing here."

"Good point." Victoria marched briskly toward the rear hall. "I'll send him a text. Either way, he'll have to wait to get in until one of us is home."

Out in the parking area, Victoria informed them that the car Nick and Ozzie shared was gone. After she climbed into the Land Rover, Victoria sent Ozzie a note. When she got a notification a minute later, she snorted. "He sent me a thumbs-up. He's all heart, isn't he?"

"You told him Nick was being questioned?" Harriet asked.

"I did." Victoria leaned back against the headrest. "Maybe now Nick will listen to me. I have to get him away from Ozzie somehow."

Harriet had to agree with Victoria. Ozzie should be rushing to Nick's aid, offering support if nothing else.

"It will all work out," Harriet said, although she wasn't sure what shape the resolution would take.

"I hope so," Victoria murmured. "Right now, I can't see a clear path forward."

"Been there. Trusting God will get you through. He's never let me down." Harriet was deeply grateful for that.

"Pray for me, please?" Victoria asked timidly.

"We will," Polly said from the back seat. "Promise."

For the rest of the ride, Victoria was silent, but her tension seemed to ease. The countryside was magnificent, with the setting sun gilding fields, stone walls, and the waves of the bay. Harriet cracked her window and breathed deeply of the sweet spring air. She'd learned to savor the peaceful moments between challenges.

With a crunch of gravel, they pulled into the parking lot at Cobble Hill Farm. "I haven't been here in years," Victoria said as she opened her door. "What a beautiful property."

"I'm the third vet to practice here," Harriet said. "It's a humbling legacy."

Victoria laughed. "I hear you. I'm the third zookeeper."

Harriet led the way to Aunt Jinny's dower cottage, cutting through the garden to the back door. Aunt Jinny had a similar setup to the vet clinic, with the doctor's office in the front and her living quarters in the rear and upstairs.

They found Aunt Jinny at the oven, pulling out the shepherd's pie. "Welcome," she said with a big smile. "Victoria, I'm so glad you could join us."

Victoria's smile was easy. "Thanks for having me." She glanced around the kitchen. "What a charming home you have."

"Thank you." Aunt Jinny gestured toward the table, already set. "Please have a seat. Harriet, there's a salad in the fridge. Polly, do you mind filling glasses with water?"

Between the three of them, they soon had dinner served. After Aunt Jinny's grace, they all dug in. Harriet didn't bring up Nick's dilemma, and neither did anyone else, including Aunt Jinny. Her kitchen was a haven, a place where Victoria could pretend for a moment that all was well.

"How are the twins?" Victoria asked.

Aunt Jinny smiled. "They're fine, thank you. Active and inquisitive, as always."

"Smart, like their parents," Harriet chimed in. "And grandmother." Her heart sank when she remembered Mango. The twins would be so sad that she'd left. "I have unhappy news, Aunt Jinny. A Border Force officer took Mango today, to send her home."

"Good for Mango," Aunt Jinny said. "I'll try to break it to the twins gently when they ask after her."

Victoria sighed. "That's the downside of caring for animals, isn't it? You can't help but get attached."

"So true," Harriet said. "I have to restrain myself from adopting them all."

"You could be like me and start a zoo. Then you can adopt them all," Victoria quipped. They all laughed. "That's how my grandfather got started, you know. Whenever he heard about an exotic animal being neglected or unwanted, he'd take it off the owner's hands. That's what I've heard, anyway."

"Percy was a very good man," Aunt Jinny said. "My father thought the world of him."

"And we Langfords all felt the same about Harold." Victoria's gaze grew distant. "I remember watching him treat animals when I was a little girl. I thought he had all the answers in his black bag. My father would say, 'We'll wait for Doc Bailey. He'll know what to do.'"

Harriet could see how this response had imbued her grandfather with mythic skills in the eyes of a child. "You're not too shabby yourself, Victoria. You take care of a lot of issues, don't you?" She thought of the well-stocked supply closet she'd seen at the zoo.

Victoria nodded. "Since we can't afford an in-house vet, yes. Dad was quite skilled too. He always assisted Harold and other vets when they attended. He took training courses, and so did I." She lifted her chin. "I'm actually certified as an assistant."

"That's wonderful," Polly said. "I'm hoping to do that as well. I've always loved animals, so I jumped at the chance to work at Cobble Hill. It's more than a passion for me. It's a calling."

"I'm lucky to have Polly," Harriet said. "I wouldn't have been able to hit the ground running without her help. She keeps the whole place impeccably organized. And all the clients and patients love her."

The color in Polly's cheeks deepened. "That's kind of you to say, Harriet." She played with her ponytail. "You should have seen Harriet with that zebra, Jinny. She was amazing."

With that remark, she gracefully deflected the conversation from herself. Harriet had noticed her assistant's modesty before. It was why she made sure to express her appreciation for Polly's work whenever the opportunity arose.

Aunt Jinny was serving apple crumble with ice cream when someone knocked on the back door.

Victoria jumped to her feet. "Is it Nick?"

Harriet would have been surprised if Nick had come here after being released, but she understood Victoria's eagerness to see her brother again.

They went through the mudroom and discovered Ozzie peering through the glass.

Victoria gasped. "I hope there isn't bad news about Nick." She opened the door. "What are you doing here?" she demanded.

Ozzie put both hands up, an unrepentant smile teasing at his lips. "You said you'd be here in your text. I was in the neighborhood and thought I'd drop by. See if you wanted a ride home."

"Oh." Victoria deflated as if the wind had been taken out of her sails. "Have you heard from Nick?"

"I haven't," Ozzie replied, not budging from the doorway, one foot over the threshold.

Harriet didn't want to be rude, even if she didn't care for the man. "Please come in, Ozzie. We're dishing up dessert if you'd like some."

Aunt Jinny raised her head when they entered the kitchen. "Hello."

Polly straightened in surprise, her brows rising.

Harriet did the introductions. "Aunt Jinny, this is Ozzie, Nick Langford's friend."

"Business partner as well." He offered his hand to shake. "Ozzie Bright. Nice to meet you." He glanced around the room. "Very charming place you have here."

"Thank you." Aunt Jinny grabbed another bowl from the cupboard. "Ice cream and crumble?"

Ozzie pulled out the chair beside Victoria. "Don't mind if I do, even if I haven't had dinner yet. Eat dessert first, right?" He elbowed Victoria, who flinched.

As they enjoyed Aunt Jinny's excellent crumble, Ozzie aimed his charm at his hostess. "Tell me about White Church Bay. Been here long?"

"For generations," Aunt Jinny said. "You'll find that's true of most locals."

Ozzie leaned closer. "Will knowing you help me make inroads?" He glanced around the table. "You ladies as well? I like to feel as if I'm part of a community."

Victoria set her jaw, but Aunt Jinny was either being polite or liked the man. Harriet couldn't tell, which spoke to her aunt's social skills.

"If you want to join the community, I recommend a little volunteer work and patronage of local businesses," Aunt Jinny said. "Those would be a good start. Let people get to know you."

Ozzie changed the subject. "I saw your clinic sign out front. Are you taking new patients? If so, I hope I can get on the list."

"I am," Aunt Jinny said. "Contact the office when we're open." She gave him the phone number.

"Ozzie, when did you meet Nick?" Harriet asked, hoping to get the man to open up. Victoria had said Nick wasn't exactly forthcoming. Maybe they could put the pieces together with Ozzie's help.

"Last year," Ozzie said. "In Germany."

Ruth Armstrong had just been in Germany. There had also been a reptile show there recently.

"Germany?" Victoria exclaimed. "I thought you lived in South Africa."

"We do. We did, I mean. I met Nick at an international trade show for home goods and accessories. He was working for a company, and I was looking to expand mine. So he came on board with me. It was a natural fit, especially since we represented different artisans and products." Ozzie's brow creased in confusion. "He hasn't told you all this?"

"He hasn't told me anything," Victoria said bitterly. "It's like his life is a big blank between the night he left and the day he returned home."

Ozzie's frown deepened. "I'm sorry to hear that. It's really up to Nick to share the details. Not that I know much either," he added hastily.

Didn't know—or didn't want to share? Harriet wished she knew. So much for her plan to glean information from Ozzie. Nick's life was a mystery, the biggest one being what exactly had happened on the sailboat that night twenty years ago.

Switching topics, Ozzie said, "I understand you've been finding some unusual reptiles, Harriet. That iguana was quite lovely. Rare, I understand."

"She is," Harriet said. "My little cousins found her hiding in the stone wall here. It was quite a surprise. Then I came across a snake the other night. Or should I say, the snake came across me. Nearly slid over my toes."

"That sounds like an interesting story," Ozzie said, his eyes dancing.

Thus encouraged, Harriet relayed the Story of the Snake, as she thought of it. It was quite humorous now, in the retelling.

The mention of Will's role made her realize they hadn't spoken today. She'd give him a call later. She had a lot to update him about.

"Where do you think they came from?" Ozzie asked. "Did they get loose from the owner's house, do you think?"

"Maybe," Harriet said. "If so, the owner hasn't come forward. In the case of the iguana, that's understandable. It's illegal to own that species. The snake is more common, although probably brought in illegally."

"Who would have thought that animals would be of interest to smugglers?" Ozzie asked.

"It's big business, apparently," Polly said. "I never had any idea how extensive until Harriet and I started digging into it. People who smuggle animals are the lowest of the low. Those poor creatures." Bright spots of indignation flamed in her cheeks.

"You're passionate and protective," Ozzie said with approval, causing Polly's color to deepen. "That's admirable." He pushed back from the table with a sigh. "I suppose I'd better be going. Lovely dessert, Jinny. It was nice to meet you."

"Great to meet you as well," Aunt Jinny said. "Thanks for stopping by."

Ozzie looked at Victoria. "Ready?"

Victoria shook her head. "I think I'll stay a little longer. If you don't mind giving me a lift home, Harriet?"

"Not a problem." Harriet was glad Victoria wasn't leaving yet. She had an idea about investigating a certain loose end, if Victoria agreed they should.

"Hold on," Victoria said. "You'll need the key." She reached for the handbag hanging from her chair back.

Ozzie, who was already halfway to the door, held up a set of keys. "Have one, thanks. Nick gave me a copy."

"Okay. See you later then." Once Ozzie was safely gone, Victoria whirled toward the remaining women. "I can't believe it. Nick gave him a key without asking me or telling me." She sighed. "Although, I suppose it is Nick's home too."

This was a perfect introduction to the subject on Harriet's mind. "Did you get a chance to check your father's will? And call the attorney, like I suggested?"

Victoria bit her lip. "I've been meaning to, but I'm barely on solid footing with Nick. I've been afraid to rock the boat." She made a face. "So to speak."

"I get that, but it would be a good idea if you had all the facts about the inheritance. What exactly did your father do legally after Nick disappeared?"

"I don't know," Victoria said, misery in every line of her posture. "I never asked. It wasn't exactly a pleasant topic to bring up.

And it would have seemed as if I only cared about the property. Dad wasn't exactly forthcoming, but who could blame him for that?"

"Some people have a real blind spot around the topic of wills," Aunt Jinny said gently. "Even very smart people who are otherwise savvy. It forces them to face the logistic aspects of their own mortality, which makes it more real than many people are comfortable with. Understandably."

"That would be Dad," Victoria agreed. "There was a will, at least. My understanding was that Nick and I were always going to split everything. Scott had money from his late parents. Dad managed the funds, and I believe they're still sitting there."

"One of my distant relatives refused to talk about 'grim subjects,' as he put it," Polly put in. "They had to search his cottage for the will." She shook her head. "Finally found it in an old tea tin. Fortunately, it was properly witnessed and signed, which kept things simpler for his six children."

"I want to do the right thing," Victoria insisted. "I'm just worried about the fate of the zoo. Nick despises it."

"A valid concern," Aunt Jinny said. "Those animals must be like family to you."

"They really are." Victoria's face brightened. "I literally grew up with so many of them. Regis. Peanut. Zippy." The lion, elephant, and zebra.

"Did the will make any stipulations about the zoo?" Aunt Jinny asked. Her late husband, Dominick, had been a lawyer, and one of his specialties had been estate law. "Such as requiring the heirs to operate it, or what would happen if one wanted to give up ownership?"

Victoria thought for a moment. "I'm not sure. Quite frankly, I glossed over most of what was said during the reading. And if Nick was presumed gone, the attorney might have skipped that part. I was so upset about my father, plus grappling with the fact that I was alone in the world." A beat. "Or so I thought."

"We'll put that aside for now," Aunt Jinny said. "If you want, I can check some legal databases and see if your father filed for presumption of death for Nick."

Victoria stared at her. "You know how to do that?"

Aunt Jinny nodded. "My late husband was an attorney. Once in a while I'd check something for him when he was swamped." She glanced at the kettle. "That will be a minute, so excuse me while I get my laptop."

"This is so nice of your aunt," Victoria said after Aunt Jinny left the room. "I suppose I could try to figure it out myself or call the attorney and ask, but this is better. I feel like I have support."

"You do," Harriet told her. She knew all too well how it felt to have one's entire future put in jeopardy. Her first month running the clinic had been marred by a case from the past that had threatened the reputation of her family and business. "Sometimes you have to buckle in and have faith the ride will smooth out."

"Good analogy," Victoria said.

Aunt Jinny returned with her laptop. "Victoria, why don't you come sit beside me?" She patted the adjacent chair. "I haven't done this for a while, so bear with me." She nodded and typed as Victoria gave her information. "Ah, here we go."

"Did you find something?" Harriet asked eagerly.

"Your father did file for a presumption of death for Nick and Scott," Aunt Jinny said. She pointed at the screen. "It was granted on that date."

Harriet poured tea and handed it around. "What does this mean for Nick?"

"I'm no attorney," Aunt Jinny warned as she added milk to her tea, "but I do know that Nick's appearance doesn't automatically reverse this. The court will have to make a determination." She leaned forward. "I'll print the case info then research the procedure."

As Aunt Jinny had said, the return of someone from being presumed dead didn't mean they were automatically entitled to any inheritances or even property they had owned. "This might seem harsh, but those left behind acted in good faith, and they shouldn't be penalized."

"I don't mind sharing," Victoria said. "That's not the problem."

Harriet knew she would likely feel the same way in Victoria's situation. "Maybe you can come to an agreement with Nick about the zoo before the property is divided." At least the required procedure in this instance would give Victoria time to resolve any issues.

"That sounds like a plan," Victoria said. "Unless he's arrested for murder." Her voice sank to a whisper. "Then everything will get even more complicated."

CHAPTER FOURTEEN

"He's still not answering my texts," Victoria said. "I wonder if I should call the station."

It was almost nine o'clock, and Harriet couldn't imagine that the police were still interviewing Nick. Surely if he'd been arrested, he would have called his sister and let her know.

"Let me try Van." Harriet placed the call over the hands-free system in the Land Rover. After a moment, they heard the sound of ringing over the line.

"Hello?" Van sounded tired.

"Van, it's Harriet," she said. "I was hoping you could tell me whether Nick Langford is still at the station."

"Um, no. He was released hours ago."

"Whew." Victoria exhaled loudly. "I'm so relieved."

"Who's that?" Van asked. "Polly?" He sounded hopeful.

"No, it's Victoria Langford. She hasn't heard from Nick, and she was getting worried."

"I thought you locked him up and threw away the key," Victoria said, her tone buoyant.

"Not at all," Van said. "He answered our questions, and we had to let him go."

Harriet tensed. *Had* to let him go. Did that mean the police still suspected Nick of foul play? She glanced at Victoria for a reaction.

"So he went home?" Victoria asked.

"I don't know," Van said. "He left with his attorney around seven. We had to wait for the lawyer to get there before we got started."

Two hours, and no word from Nick to his sister. Harriet felt a charge of anger on Victoria's behalf. Surely he must know that she was waiting to hear from him. That she was worried about him. Perhaps he had fallen out of the habit of letting someone know where he was and what he was doing, but if he truly wanted to form a relationship with his sister, he'd better get into that habit. And fast.

"Anything else?" Harriet asked Victoria softly. When she shook her head, she raised her voice. "Thanks, Van. We'll let you go. Have a good night."

"You too." Van hung up.

Victoria grabbed her own phone, jabbed at the screen a few times, then pressed it to her ear. "Pick up, Nick. Pick up." Her nose wrinkled, and Harriet assumed she'd gotten her brother's voice mail. "Nick, it's me. I hope you're at home. I'm on my way." She disconnected with a grunt of annoyance. "Why isn't he talking to me?"

Harriet was beginning to see a pattern. Nick had been refusing to communicate with Victoria all along. He'd had nothing to say about the netsuke being stolen, or where he had been for twenty years. Why he'd run away and left his family believing he was dead. And now, after being taken to the station for questioning about Scott's death, he had neither reached out to Victoria nor responded to her attempts to communicate.

His actions—or lack thereof—painted a picture, and it wasn't a pretty one. How could Victoria and Nick rebuild their relationship and manage their inheritance if he refused to talk to her? To answer questions and face the pain and distress his actions had caused?

"You know what?" Victoria mused. "Some of what Dad said over the years is making sense to me now. He never got over losing Nick. He had deep regrets about how he handled their relationship. Nick would do the same thing back then—shut down and refuse to communicate. Dad would get even more heavy-handed in response. Obviously, that didn't work."

"My heart goes out to you all," Harriet said. "Families can be so hard." In this case, it sounded like father and son had loved each other but hadn't been able to talk to each other. She said a quick, silent prayer that Victoria and Nick could forge a healthier path together.

Victoria's vehicle was the only one in the lot. "Ozzie's not here." She squinted at the house. "No lights on. Seems they're both gone."

"Maybe they're together," Harriet suggested. That would mean Nick had called Ozzie rather than his sister. "I'll walk you in."

As Victoria had thought, no one was home. After a scan of the downstairs rooms, they went into the conservatory. Victoria went to the genet cage and counted them. "All the remaining ones are accounted for. I still can't believe one got out. I'm worried another will disappear."

"That would be awful." The nocturnal creatures were active at the moment, and Harriet smiled at their antics. After a few minutes, she reluctantly pulled herself away. "I'd better get going. I've got an early morning."

Just then, they heard the rear door open and shut and the scrape of footsteps in the hall. Victoria's face lit up. "I wonder if that's Nick." She went to the doorway. "Nick. Thank goodness. We're in here."

Nick looked tired. His shoulders were slumped, and he had bluish half-moons under his eyes. "What's up?"

"Nothing much," Victoria said. "I had dinner with Harriet, and she brought me home. How about you? How did it go with the police? Where have you been?"

Nick's eyes widened. "Whoa. What's with all the questions?"

"The police said you left hours ago," Victoria told him. "Why didn't you let me know how it went? I've been worried sick."

He set his jaw. "I was there for a long time. It was awful. Then I went to see a friend, okay? I do have a few friends left around here, you know."

Victoria crossed her arms. "What friend? Seriously, Nick, you're so blasé about the whole thing. Why am I not a priority?" Tears glittered in her eyes. "Oh, that's right. I never have been."

Harriet took a step toward the door. She didn't need to be a witness to a family argument. Victoria touched Harriet's arm, a silent request for her to stay. Uneasy, Harriet shifted from foot to foot, tempted to bolt.

"Wow," Nick said. "That's below the belt. My leaving had nothing to do with you."

"How could it?" Victoria sounded bitter. "I was only five, a little kid who adored her big brother. You didn't care how it would affect me. I cried myself to sleep for months." Her chin went up. "So why did you come back now?"

Her brother's face flushed a deep red. "I thought it was time—"

"Time to waltz in and take over from your little sister?"

His flush deepened. "Of course not. I have regrets, you know." He swallowed. "Especially about Dad." Then his expression hardened. "Besides, this place is half mine. Why shouldn't I be here?"

Victoria's broken laugh was painful to hear. "Now we get to the truth. You're here for the estate. Well, guess what? It's not yours. Not anymore. So quit giving out keys to strangers."

Nick took a step back, a stunned expression on his face. "What do you mean? Dad said the property would be split evenly." He frowned. "Did you do something to him, influence his mind somehow? Tell him to cut me out? I'll sue—"

"I didn't do a thing." Her lips pressed into a hard line. "Dad had you declared dead. Which means that you need to apply to the court to get your inheritance back. They might not give it to you. They often don't. He acted in good faith." A pause. "Unlike you."

At this last verbal blow, Nick spun and charged out of the room. A moment later, Harriet heard a door slam.

Victoria burst into tears, her whole body shaking. Harriet put an arm around her, murmuring soothing words. "I didn't mean that," Victoria sobbed. "He must hate me now."

"He doesn't hate you," Harriet said automatically. He had simply encountered reality in a way that probably felt like running into a brick wall. Whatever Nick's feelings toward his father or sister, he had expected to pick up where he left off, as heir to Langford Hall. The plans he and Ozzie had to operate their business here were now on hold, perhaps permanently, if the court ruled against him.

What was worse, in Harriet's mind, was the damage that would be done to the relationship between brother and sister if they went the legal route. How could they coexist here if the judge awarded half the estate to Nick? On the other hand, if that didn't happen, Nick would probably never speak to his sister again. Victoria would lose him for good—for real this time.

Victoria grabbed a tissue from a box on a table. "Sorry you had to hear that, Harriet. I shouldn't have stopped you from leaving." Her laugh was shaky. "I'm a coward, for sure."

"It's okay." Harriet thought it was good someone else had been there. After all, how well did they know Nick? Not at all, if she was being honest. For all they knew, he might have reacted violently if Victoria had been alone. *Like he might have with Scott?* "It's a really, really difficult situation. I wish I could do more to help."

"You are helping. I don't know how I'd get through this without friends." Victoria dabbed at her eyes and then blew her nose. "If only he weren't keeping so many secrets. About where he was all these years. What happened on the sailboat. Even where he went tonight. How am I supposed to trust him when I don't know him?"

"I don't see how you can," Harriet said. "He has to come clean and confront the past before you two can move on. It's not fair for him to step in and act like he can pick up where he left off."

"You're right," Victoria said. "I'm not that little girl anymore, agreeable and easy to push around. He'd better learn that once and for all."

Harriet drove home through the quiet countryside, her thoughts consumed by the scene she had just witnessed. What a tangle. A joyful homecoming between long-separated siblings had been complicated by unanswered questions, distrust, and an uncertain future.

The power to rectify most of it lay in Nick's hands. If he thought he could bury the past by ignoring it, he was mistaken. Besides the pressing issues around the inheritance and their cousin's death, Victoria had been badly hurt by his disappearance and ensuing silence. Not to mention the fact that he hadn't reconciled with his father before he died. That was a situation that could never be made right.

He needed to rebuild his relationship with Victoria. Or at least try.

It was as if the siblings stood on two sides of a gulf they couldn't bridge. Harriet said a prayer that they would be able to, somehow. That they could face the road ahead with mutual respect, love, and understanding.

Speaking of relationships, she needed to call Will. When she parked at home, her phone read ten o'clock.

As she walked inside, she sent him a text. Too late to talk?

Not at all. Still up.

Give me five.

Harriet checked on Charlie and Maxwell, filled a glass with water, and then headed to her reading nook. "Hey," she said when he answered. Her pulse rate had risen a notch at the sound of his voice, she noticed. Will certainly had an effect on her, even over the phone.

"How are you? Any more encounters with snakes?" He chuckled.

Harriet shuddered. "Not yet, thankfully. Speaking of Slippery, he or she is safely housed at Moorland Zoo." She launched into an update, taking Will through the new developments. Border Force taking Mango. Nick being taken in for questioning. Aunt Jinny's research, a genet going missing. The confrontation between Nick and Victoria.

"Wow," Will said. "I can't leave you alone for a minute."

"Seriously, it was a lot for one day," Harriet agreed. "I'm pretty wiped out."

"I should probably visit Victoria," Will said. "I feel remiss that I haven't gone over since the sailboat was found."

"That would be great," Harriet said. "She could use a little pastoral counsel, I'm sure. It's such a confusing time for her. Happy but also sad and difficult." She had another thought. "Maybe Nick will talk to you. He must be equally confused."

"He might," Will said. "I'll play it by ear. See if we can establish a rapport."

"Awesome." Harriet admired Will's sensitivity and insight, how he made people feel supported and heard. He'd done that for her ever since they'd first met. "You're the best."

Will laughed. "Please call whenever you want. I can use the ego boost."

Harriet smiled. "Anytime." She changed the subject. "Remember my goal to try new things this spring to break out of my rut? Like the boat tour?" Look how that had turned out. Harriet hoped her next activity wouldn't launch an avalanche of consequences.

"Do you have something else in mind?" Will asked. "I'm free on Saturday."

"Perfect." Harriet had a light morning schedule, so she would be off most of the day. "Polly and I talked about taking a hike on the moors. I've heard they're gorgeous in the spring."

"Spectacular, actually. I know a good loop up to some standing stones that would take us a few hours to walk. We can take a picnic. On the way home, we'll stop for dinner at a great old pub I know."

The outing sounded wonderful. "Is it a tough trail?" While Harriet was in pretty good shape, it had been a while since she'd gone hiking. She didn't want to bite off too much her first time out.

"Intermediate, I'd say. There are some hills, but nothing too steep. I'll send you a link to a website that will explain better than I can." After a pause, he said, "Think we should ask Polly and Van to come along?"

"Maybe," Harriet said. "Polly told me they've agreed to be friends and will be hanging out with us sometimes."

"That's a start, for sure," Will said. "I still think they make a great couple."

"They do," Harriet agreed. "And maybe they'll get back together at some point." She thought for a moment. "I'll ask Polly about the hike, and we can take it from there."

"Sounds like a plan. Either way, we're going to have a great time."

"I'll ask her tomorrow," Harriet said. Hopefully, Polly and Van would join them. The four of them always had a great time.

Perhaps it would be good for Van and Polly to remember that.

CHAPTER FIFTEEN

Coffee mug in hand, Harriet stepped out into the tender spring morning, the sky now clear after heavy rain during the night. Droplets sparkled in the grass, and birds chirped busily in the trees and bushes. Charlie took a few tentative steps, shaking her paws free of water, while Maxwell nosed in the bushes, no doubt hoping to pick up a bunny trail.

More daffodils were popping up, and the first tulips were coming into bloom. Harriet inhaled briny sea air, her heart lifting. Who could be in a bad mood on a day like this?

Polly came around the corner of the building, her ponytail bobbing. "Thought I'd find you out here." She inhaled deeply. "What a gorgeous day. Too bad our work is inside."

"I hope it's this nice on Saturday," Harriet said, then winced. She hadn't meant to dive right into the topic of the hike.

"Why's that?" Polly sipped from her thermos.

She might as well come clean now. "Will and I talked about going on a hike on the moors. Up to some standing stones, he said."

"I know that trail. It's a good one. You can see for miles up there, and the stones themselves are fascinating." Polly peered closely at Harriet. "What is it?"

"Well, we were wondering if you'd like to go with us." Harriet lowered her voice. "And maybe ask Van."

"Van?" Polly fastened on the key point. "You want him to go with us?"

"If you're comfortable with it," Harriet said. "The four of us always have fun, and Van could bring his snake catcher to protect us."

Polly shook her head, laughing. "That might be useful, the way things are going."

"Does that mean you're okay with the idea?" Harriet asked, seizing the moment.

"I am." Polly pursed her lips. "We're friends, right?" She took another sip from her cup. "Speaking of snakes, I have someone I want you to meet."

Harriet's heart leaped. "Someone found another stray?"

"Not that I know of. I was referring to one of my brothers' friends in town." Polly nodded toward the village. "Eddie might know something about smuggling in the area. He's had snakes and lizards for years, and he has tons of connections in the reptile-enthusiast community."

"That's a brilliant idea," Harriet said. "There's a lot I don't know about reptile ownership and their networks." Mango and Slippery must have come from somewhere. Although Border Force was supposedly investigating, Officer Crosby hadn't been especially responsive. Except to take Mango away, she remembered with a pang.

"We could drop in on him after work," Polly suggested. "Maybe grab a bite to eat."

Which meant Harriet wouldn't have to worry about dinner after a busy day. "I'm in. Where should we go?"

"The Crow's Nest," Polly said with a smile. "I'm in the mood for toad-in-the-hole."

After the clinic closed, Harriet and Polly walked down to the village. It was too nice a day to drive, and Harriet enjoyed the chance to stretch her legs after months of being cooped up by the winter weather.

Eddie lived in the lower village, in one of the houses tucked in a neat row. Polly rang the bell, and a moment later they heard footsteps clattering down a set of stairs.

A young man with a mop of curly hair and a goatee opened the door and smiled. "Hello, Polly. And Dr. Bailey, right? I'm Eddie."

"Please, call me Harriet. Nice to meet you."

They followed Eddie up a steep staircase to his flat, which was one large room with a bath and bedroom off it. In one corner of the space stood several cages, with lights and heat lamps hung around them. The furnishings were comfortable, if simple, and a mug and a half-empty plate sat on the kitchenette table.

"We interrupted your dinner," Polly said. "I'm sorry."

"No worries," Eddie assured her. "Want to meet the gang?"

"I do." Harriet had already moved closer to the cages, fascinated.

"This is Monty," Eddie announced, extracting a three-foot-long spotted lizard from a cage. "He's a monitor lizard. Give him a pat. He's quite friendly."

Harriet ran her hand along his back, the reptile docile in his owner's hands. "Have you had him long?"

Eddie rubbed Monty under his chin. "Since he was a baby. I bought him at the York show they have every year. The next one is in a couple of weeks."

"Do you ever go to Europe for shows?" Harriet asked. "I heard there was a big one in Germany recently."

Eddie nodded. "I was there. Some dealers I know were selling, and I helped them out."

Polly admired Monty. "Did you hear about the smugglers they arrested?"

Eddie gave a little groan. "Those crooks give reptile ownership a bad name. The sellers I know do everything by the book. A creature like Monty here? You want to socialize him young. Wild monitors can be dangerous. They bite and scratch, and the cuts can get infected."

He urged the lizard back into his cage and moved to the next. A long brown snake with tan patches, about as big around as Eddie's forearm, was curled up inside. "This is Prunella. She's a ball python." He removed Prunella from the cage and allowed the snake to curl around his neck and arm. He chuckled at the shock on his guests' faces. "She's totally harmless. She eats mice, not people."

As a vet and animal lover, Harriet admired Prunella. She couldn't imagine ever owning a snake though.

"She's beautiful," Polly said. She leaned back when Eddie made as though to hand the snake to her. "That's okay. I'll love her from a distance."

Eddie laughed. "Lots of people feel that way." He gazed into the snake's eyes, her head in his hand. "They don't know you like I do, Pruny." He placed her inside her cage. "Ball pythons are one of the most popular snakes because they're so calm and easy to care for. We sold a lot of them in Germany." He secured the latch. "Want to see some pictures from the event?"

Photos from the event might give them some answers. "Sure. That'd be great."

"One more buddy to show you first." Eddie beamed with pride. "My chameleon, Curtis." He moved to a cage on a table, equipped with tree branches, plants, and rocks.

Curtis was green with yellow stripes on his back. Eddie took him out, and Curtis perched on his hand. "They don't like a lot of handling. He's used to me though."

"Very handsome," Harriet said. "Does he change colors?"

"Sometimes," Eddie said. "Temperature can trigger it. So can stress, which I try to avoid." He gently returned Curtis to the cage. "I'll show you the photos on my tablet."

They went over to the table and sat, Eddie pushing aside his cup and plate. He turned on a tablet and scrolled to the photo library.

"Did you hear about the rock iguana we found?" Harriet asked.

Eddie gaped at her. "What? No. Around here?" He placed the tablet on a stand, where they could see the screen.

Polly already had her phone out. "Here's a photo. We called her Mango."

The young man took the phone and studied the photo, his expression both fascinated and horrified. "That species is rare. It's illegal to capture them."

"We know," Harriet said. "We took her to Moorland Zoo to be cared for until the Border Force could collect her. She's being sent back to the Bahamas."

His nod was decisive. "Good." His brows drew together. "Where do you think she came from?"

"That's the mystery," Harriet said. "She must have escaped from a smuggler or a private owner. Either way, it's fortunate we found her. The temperatures are still cold at night."

Eddie shuddered. "I don't even want to think about it." He leaned forward. "If you want, I can ask around, see if I can turn up any leads. I'll be discreet, I promise. Last thing I want is to get beat up."

"Would smugglers do that?" Harriet asked, appalled.

"Or worse. There's a lot of money in smuggling rare animals. That iguana is worth tens of thousands." Eddie focused on the tablet. "Anyway, this shot shows the venue."

He scrolled through the photos, showing them the variety of reptiles that had been available. Some images were bird's-eye views of the exhibition hall and the crowd.

Something caught Harriet's eye. "Wait. Can you enlarge this photo? That woman looks familiar." Eddie did as she requested.

"It's Ruth," Polly said. "From the Happy Cup."

Eddie enlarged the photo even more. "I think you're right. I saw her there the other day."

"Who is she with, I wonder?" Harriet mused. The man she was talking to faced away from the camera, so all she could see was the back of his head—and he was wearing a cap.

"Can't tell," Polly said. "Too bad."

Eddie's gaze flicked between Harriet and Polly. "You think it means something that Ruth was there?"

"I don't know," Harriet said. "She's also an animal activist. Maybe that's why she went."

He frowned. "Yeah, we had a few protesters there. They mean well, but they don't understand. We can't simply let these reptiles go.

They'd die left to their own devices in the wild." After a beat, he added, "I am on board with cracking down on stealing from local populations, though. That's why we advocate for ethical breeding in captivity. People get to have healthy reptiles as pets, and the wild ones are safe."

"That's a great approach," Harriet said with approval. "By the way, I also found a loose sand boa on the cliff walk the other night."

"You're kidding," Eddie exclaimed. "What is going on around here?"

"That's what I'd like to know," Harriet said. "I hope you and your friends can help."

Founded in 1636, the Crow's Nest was located deep in the maze of lanes that made up the village. Harriet had been there plenty of times since moving to the area, and she still had to check her route to make sure she didn't get lost.

Even on a Wednesday evening, the place was busy, with patrons at the bar and tables or clustered near the dartboards. They managed to grab an empty booth along the wall.

"Toad-in-the-hole looks good," Harriet said, watching a server carry plates to a nearby table. What was not to like about sausages and Yorkshire pudding? "I'll get that too."

After two glasses of root beer were delivered, they sat back to relax and chat. "Eddie was really helpful," Polly said. "Don't you think?"

"He was." Harriet sipped her root beer. "If he puts the word out to his network, someone might know something. Mango and

Slippery didn't simply appear out of thin air, after all." There was also the risk that any owners with illicit reptiles would go further underground. But she'd learned to follow leads as they presented themselves, trusting that the truth would eventually be revealed.

Polly's brows rose as she gazed past Harriet to another table. "Well, there's trouble." As Harriet started to twist in her seat, she whispered, "No. Not yet." After a few more seconds, she said, "Now. They're not looking."

Harriet cautiously glanced over her shoulder to take in the room behind her. Ozzie and Nick sat at a table with two women—Ruth and Cassandra, Harriet's client who owned the gorgeous Bengal cat.

"Must be a reunion," Harriet said. "Nick went to school with Ruth and Cassandra. Last night, when I took Victoria home, Nick said he'd been visiting an old friend. I wonder if he meant one of them."

"They seem pretty chummy now," Polly noted as laughter broke out at the foursome's table. "Must be nice for Nick to connect with old friends."

"Except one spends part of her time protesting his family's zoo," Harriet pointed out. The server was approaching with plates, so she sat back.

"Toad-in-a-hole," the server said, setting the plates on the table. "Careful, they're hot." After making sure they were all set, he hurried away.

They said grace then dug in.

"Nick doesn't like the zoo either," Polly reminded Harriet. "Maybe he's bonding with Ruth over it."

Harriet groaned. "Don't say that. Poor Victoria." She took a bite, the savory flavor of sausage and eggy pudding blending perfectly. "This is so good."

"Isn't it?" Polly forked up another bite with enthusiasm. Her phone dinged, and she checked it. "It's a text from Eddie."

"Asking for a date?" Harriet teased. She wouldn't be surprised. Eddie was about Polly's age.

"No." Polly rolled her eyes. "He said a reptile-owner club is getting together Monday evening. You and I are invited to attend and see if anyone has any information. I'm game if you are."

"That might be a good idea," Harriet said. "Why don't you get the details and tell him we'll try to make it." Barring a vet emergency, they should be able to go.

Dessert was sticky toffee pudding. Afterward, Harriet popped into the ladies' room.

Ruth and Cassandra stood by the sinks. Cassandra was putting on lipstick while Ruth gushed, "I love his accent. It's *so* dreamy."

Cassandra capped her lipstick. "He's a cutie all right. Very thoughtful too."

Ruth glanced over and noticed Harriet. "Hello. How are you?"

"Fine, thank you," Harriet said. "Nice to see you both." She nodded a greeting at Cassandra. "How's Butterscotch?"

Still staring into the mirror at her reflection, the Bengal's owner beamed. "Doing great, thanks. Such a love."

"Harriet," Ruth said, her brow furrowed, "you're friends with Victoria Langford, right? You've been at the zoo a lot."

Wondering where Ruth was going with this, Harriet tensed. "I've been filling in while her usual vet is on vacation."

"That's what Nick said." Ruth folded her arms. "Maybe you can talk sense into his sister. She's treating Nick like he doesn't belong here. As if the property isn't half his."

Harriet took a step back. "That's not my place, Ruth. I can't comment on their private business."

"Um, yeah," Cassandra said hesitantly. "Ruth, why don't we—"

Ruth tossed her head with a snort. "I normally wouldn't either, but this is too unfair. She told Nick that he can't locate his company operations at Langford Hall." Her eyes flashed with annoyance. "And she also told Ozzie that he's not welcome to stay at the house anymore. She's kicking him out."

CHAPTER SIXTEEN

Secretly, Harriet was proud of Victoria for setting boundaries. She was letting her brother and his friend know that they couldn't push her around. However, this was not the time, place, or audience for her to express these thoughts.

Rather than responding, she gestured. "I'm sorry. I need to—"

Ruth's chin went up in the air. "Ready, Cassandra? Let's go." Without waiting for her friend, she swept out of the restroom, the door swinging shut behind her.

Cassandra shrugged, her expression apologetic. "Sorry about that. Ruth is rather outspoken at times."

"So I've noticed." Harriet forced a smile. "It's okay."

"Have a good night." Cassandra picked up her handbag and left.

On the walk home, safely away from listening ears, Harriet filled Polly in on the encounter in the ladies' room. "I'm amazed that Victoria was able to do those things," she confided. "She was so conflicted last time I talked to her. She didn't want to put her foot down—"

"But she was forced to," Polly finished for her. "I don't blame her. They were basically steamrolling her in her own home. Remember how they were poking around the zoo for a place to put the business? She should have been involved in that conversation."

"You'd think so. In any event, the battle lines have been drawn," Harriet said. "I'm sure Nick will take the case to court."

"Unless Victoria can come to an agreement with him first," Polly said.

Harriet thought back to the conversation with Victoria. "She wants to. She also wants to make sure the zoo isn't threatened by his plans for the property, should they share its use."

Polly lived in the upper village, so Harriet walked her home and then went the rest of the way alone. At the junction of the cliff path, she hesitated. Should she walk the road, so she was less likely to encounter another snake or iguana? Or the path, so she could help if one was out there?

The cliff path, she decided. There were actually more people out there than on the roads at this time of night. And if there were other runaway reptiles in White Church Bay, she wanted to find them.

Harriet took out her phone, ready to use the flashlight app if needed. Otherwise, she'd let her eyes adjust. A surprising amount of light reflected off the sea, which lay like a sheet of dark silver to her left. She could hear the shushing of the waves against the shore and the chirp of nightjars as they swooped, hunting.

Harriet took a deep inhale of salty air as she paused to take in the view. The coast was ever-changing, in different seasons, weather, and times of day. She enjoyed every mood, every facet of its beauty.

Voices came along the path from the direction of the village. She waited for them to pass, not wanting people on her heels.

The group included two couples, and she immediately recognized one of the male voices. Ozzie.

"Bit of a tough break, but it will all come right," he was saying as they drew closer. "Wait and see. You've got your lucky charm."

"What's that?" one of the women asked with a laugh.

"Me, of course," Ozzie said with pride. "I'm an up-and-comer. This time next year, everyone will know who Bright and Langford are."

"You mean Langford and Bright," snapped the other man. She recognized Nick's voice. "That's how we registered."

Ozzie laughed. "So we did. Don't get your—hello. Someone's here on the path."

Harriet gave them a wave. "It's just me, Harriet. Enjoying an evening stroll."

"Why, Harriet," Ruth said. "You're popping up everywhere."

"I could say the same about you." Harriet injected humor into her reply. "It's a small village."

"So it is." Ozzie pretended to tip an invisible hat. "Have a good evening."

The foursome ambled past Harriet and continued down the path. Soon laughter and shouts drifted back to Harriet. They were having fun, she realized, a little wistfully. Saturday's ramble couldn't come fast enough.

The next afternoon, Harriet was inoculating a cow at Kettlewell Farm when Polly called. "I need to take this," she told George Kettlewell, who was assisting. His farm was one of the largest in the area, and Harriet had been pleased when he'd stayed with the clinic.

George nodded agreement, so Harriet stripped off her glove to answer. "Hello, Polly. What's up?"

"Sorry to bother you," Polly said. "I wanted to let you know that the dentist was able to schedule me, so I'll be leaving shortly. I'll have the calls forwarded to your cell phone." Polly had been trying to get a loose filling examined.

"Thanks for letting me know," Harriet said. "Anything else?"

"No, it's been quiet here. There's nothing on your schedule this afternoon when you're done with Kettlewell. I also got the paperwork done."

"Thanks. I hope everything goes well." She ended the call, tucked the phone into her pocket, and put the glove back on, resolutely putting aside her curiosity about whether anything else had happened at Langford Hall. George and his cows deserved her full attention.

Once she completed the vaccinations, the herd was turned out to graze. Then Harriet and George talked about his operation over a cup of tea. More than a dozen calves had been born this past winter, and George was gearing up for another breeding season.

As they discussed bovine health, the cost of feed, and market conditions for milk, Harriet curbed her impatience. Serving George's farm in her capacity as vet was her job, her responsibility. Everything else had to wait. Even a friend's troubles.

Once she was back in the Beast, Harriet checked her phone. She'd missed a call from Victoria, which she immediately returned.

"Harriet." Victoria sounded breathless. "I'm so glad you returned my call. Is there any possibility you can swing by in half an hour or so? My attorney is coming to meet with me about Nick and... everything."

Langford Hall wasn't far from Kettlewell Farm. "Are you sure you want me there?"

"Definitely. You've been such a support. I tried Polly but couldn't reach her."

"She's at a dentist appointment." How could she say no? Her heart went out to Victoria, who was basically alone in the world. At least until things were resolved with her brother—and they seemed to be headed in the opposite direction.

Harriet glanced down at her clothes. "I'm warning you, I'm dressed for the farmyard, not a meeting."

"I've been working out in the zoo. She'll have to take us as we are."

"Sounds good. See you in a few." Harriet carried shoes in the Land Rover, so at least she wouldn't be tracking barnyard soil through the beautiful manor.

Lorelai Wickham was a gracious woman in her fifties, sleekly dressed in a suit and heels, with her chestnut hair in an elegant French twist. "Dr. Bailey, it's so nice to meet you," she said, her voice low and soothing. "I've always heard good things about Cobble Hill."

"Thank you," Harriet said. Since the attorney lived an hour away in York, that meant the clinic's reputation was quite widespread.

The attorney gestured. "Why don't we get started?"

They took seats at a table in the study, a large room furnished with bookshelves, an impressive desk, and cases holding valuable, animal-themed art. Harriet noticed the netsuke collection, miniature and finely carved figures from Japan.

Victoria had a copy of the will, which she shared with Harriet. "I know you took me through this after Dad died, Lorelai. Unfortunately, I didn't retain much."

"That's perfectly normal," Lorelai assured her. "You mentioned on the phone that your brother has returned unexpectedly." She folded her hands under her chin. "Why don't you fill me in?"

Victoria gave her an overview of the situation twenty years before and how the family hadn't heard from Nick since. "Then he showed up one day last week, thinking he could simply step back into the picture."

Lorelai tapped her pen against the will. "He *is* named as a beneficiary, with the estate shared equally."

"That's all well and good," Victoria said. "Except my dad had him declared dead seven years after the shipwreck." She opened a folder. "I have the documents right here."

Lorelai's eyes widened. "Is that so? Your father never updated his will or informed the office about this. That I know of. It wasn't my case at the time. It belonged to my father, who has since retired." Shaking her head, she leafed through Victoria's folder. "This all looks to be in order. I need to call the office." She pushed back from the desk, picked up her phone, and walked a few paces away.

Harriet and Victoria exchanged glances. "This explains a lot," Victoria said. "I didn't know about the declaration of death, and neither did the attorney's office. Thank goodness for Aunt Jinny."

"I'm glad she could help." Harriet wondered if anyone would have found the filing. It was odd that Marshall hadn't updated his attorney—or his will—but many people had trouble dealing with painful topics.

Victoria glanced at a nearby display case, which held a number of small animal-themed statues. Her eyes narrowed, and she got up and went to study the contents more closely.

After a moment, she returned to her seat, but before Harriet could question her, Lorelai bustled back to the table.

"All right," the lawyer said as she sat. "My assistant will make sure our files are updated. With the declaration in force, your brother will need to petition the court to request his share of the inheritance. They have discretion whether to award that, seeing as you acted in good faith upon the death of your father."

"That's what I understand," Victoria said. "What if I want to divide the estate?"

Lorelai pursed her lips. "That is up to you. We would draw up papers distributing ownership, with details of the assets to be transferred. Joint heirs often sell and distribute the proceeds, or one buys out the other. This property is large enough that the land could be split, although the house itself holds a good chunk of value."

Victoria's shoulders sagged. "What does that mean for the zoo? It occupies most of the acreage."

Lorelai toyed with her pen. "Again, you would have to come to an agreement. Maybe buy out his ownership?"

"I don't have that kind of money." Victoria's lower lip trembled. "Maybe doing the right thing won't work."

"Could he help you run it?" Lorelai's voice was gentle.

"Nick doesn't like the zoo," Harriet explained. "There isn't anything in the will that requires the property to remain whole, is there?"

"I'm afraid not." Lorelai folded her hands. "Any other questions?"

Victoria shook her head. "Not right now. I'll have to think about next steps."

Lorelai began to gather her things. "Call me anytime with questions, okay? If you decide to split the property, we can meet and discuss the implications then come up with the best way to proceed. I'm here to help protect your interests, Victoria."

"Thank you. I appreciate your help." Despite her words, the young woman appeared troubled. Harriet couldn't blame her. There was no easy fix for her situation.

All three women rose from their seats. "Nice to meet you, Dr. Bailey." Lorelai opened her leather portfolio and pulled out a business card, which she handed to Harriet. "In case my services are ever needed."

Harriet accepted the card, although she already had an attorney for legal services, the one her grandfather had used.

As they moved toward the door, Victoria showing Lorelai out, Nick entered the room, followed by Ruth. "What's going on?" he asked.

Victoria flushed, her gaze darting from person to person. "Nick. What are you doing here?"

Her brother's chin went up. "None of your business." His brows drew together as he stared at Lorelai with a hostile expression. "Who are you?"

At his tone, Ruth backed up a couple of steps then hesitated, clearly uncertain about whether to stay or go. As another reluctant witness to a family argument, Harriet sympathized.

The attorney took Nick's aggression in stride. "I'm Lorelai Wickham. Your father's attorney, and now, your sister's."

"Attorney?" Nick sounded both surprised and worried. "Did you handle the will?"

Lorelai nodded. "My firm did. As a named beneficiary, you'd normally be entitled to see a copy. However, I'm not prepared to give you one at the moment. You should retain your own counsel."

"What do you mean?" Nick demanded.

Victoria answered his question. "Remember what I told you? That Dad had you declared dead? According to the law, you don't exist. So you can't inherit."

"Seriously?" Nick took a step forward. "But I'm right here. Obviously, I exist."

"I need to get to another appointment," Lorelai said smoothly as she edged past the siblings. "I'll show myself out. Call me anytime, Victoria."

In the doorway, Ruth dodged out of Lorelai's way. She glared at Lorelai as she went by, as if battle lines had been drawn and Ruth and Nick were on the same side. Lorelai's gaze remained straight ahead, as if she didn't even see Ruth.

Harriet supposed the alliance made sense. Ruth and Nick both despised the zoo.

Ruth charged forward, arms swinging. "He's your brother. Why are you doing this to him? This place should be half his. It's the right thing to do."

As if Ruth hadn't spoken, Victoria marched over to the display case she'd been examining earlier. "I have a question for you, Nick. Where is the gold giraffe statue?"

CHAPTER SEVENTEEN

Nick joined his sister beside the case. "Gold giraffe? What are you talking about?"

Victoria jabbed a finger at an empty space on one shelf. "The pure-gold, fourteenth-century giraffe. Worth about ten thousand pounds."

Ruth gasped. "The giraffe is gone? It was my favorite back when I used to visit." She bent close to peer through the glass, as if the statue were simply hiding.

"It wasn't me, Vic," Nick insisted. "I wouldn't take something and not tell you."

"Uh-huh." Victoria's tone was knowing. "What about the netsuke?"

"I didn't take those. Scott did. I already told you." Nick ran a hand over his hair, his eyes darting around the room. When he met Harriet's gaze, he flinched.

Victoria glared at her brother. "You've told me a lot of things—wait. That's not true. You've barely said a word. Why you ran away. Why you stayed away without a word to your family. And why you came back. Those are all questions I need answers to, Nick. And you're the only one who can give them to me."

Her brother made a show of looking at his phone. "We can talk later. I have to go." To Ruth, he said, "Wait here while I get my laptop. It's in my room."

Victoria ran after him. "Where are you going? When will you be back?"

"If you must know, we found a site for the business in the village. Our new shipment is coming in today." He disappeared through the doorway.

Victoria faced Ruth. "What's your role in all this?"

Ruth smiled. "I'm their first employee, in charge of the office. I'm doing the bookkeeping, answering the phone, checking over paperwork from the shipments. Whatever they need."

"Congrats." Harriet remembered Ruth mentioning her desire for a new job at the Happy Cup. Although she wasn't working with animals as she'd wished, she seemed enthusiastic about the position. "Where's the office?"

Ruth mentioned a street on the outskirts of White Church Bay. Harriet had driven through the area, which featured warehouses, small factories, and other business establishments.

"Well," Ruth said, waving a hand, "I'd better go meet Nick. See you later." She wandered out of the room.

Victoria closed the study door behind Ruth. "I can't *believe* this."

Harriet thought her friend's exclamation covered it all. Seeking a subject they might be able to do something about, she motioned toward the case. "Do you want to report the giraffe missing to the police?"

Victoria rubbed a hand over her face. "I can't. What if Nick did take it? He's in enough trouble over the shipwreck."

Harriet wondered if his explanation about the day the sailboat sank had satisfied the authorities. According to the police, Scott had suffered a head injury, and they wanted to know what had caused it.

Harriet tried the cabinet door. "It's locked. Where do you keep the key?"

"In the safe, with the others," Victoria said. She went behind the desk and lifted a painting off the wall. A square metal door was inserted into the wall.

"You know," Harriet said, "Nick's not the only one who might have taken the giraffe."

"You mean Ozzie?" Victoria's eyes were wide. "I didn't think of that." She spun the combination. "We also keep valuable jewelry, Dad's watch, and other heirlooms in here."

"I know you don't want to get Nick in trouble, but I think you should tell Van about the missing giraffe. He can put it on a list so if it shows up at a dealer, they'll know it's stolen."

Victoria opened the safe door. "Maybe I should do that. Put people on notice that I'm not going to be fleeced. Not by anyone."

"Good for you," Harriet said.

Victoria began to sort through the contents of the safe. "Everything's here, thank goodness." She picked up a set of jingling keys. "These are staying with me until I get the combination changed."

Harriet nodded toward the display case. "Maybe you should change those locks. If it was Ozzie, he could have made a copy of the key."

Victoria's shoulders slumped. "I didn't even think of that." She flipped through a card file on the desk. "I'm calling the locksmith right now."

Harriet pulled out her phone. "I'll call Van."

Harriet stayed at Langford Hall until Van arrived. As she had come to expect from him, the detective constable took the missing giraffe seriously. He assured them that he would add it to the stolen-property lists the police maintained. He also offered to notify various local dealers and shops to be on the lookout for it.

As Harriet drove home in the fading light, she realized she was exhausted and starving. She mentally reviewed the contents of her refrigerator and pantry. Both were pretty bare, and she remembered using the last of the milk in her morning coffee. She ought to stop at the big supermarket near the motorway and pick up a few things. That would be easier than visiting Galloway's General Store in the lower village. For one thing, she could drive practically up to the door.

Harriet was grabbing her wallet in the grocery store parking lot when her phone rang with a call from Jason. "Hey, friend. How's your vacation?"

Jason laughed. "It's precisely what the doctor ordered. I'm having a great time rambling around county trails and taking in sights I never have time for. Museums, concerts, art shows."

"Staycation?" Harriet asked.

"Exactly. Anyway, that's not why I called. My contact at the Wildlife Crimes Unit sent me a note. They're still working on setting up a flight for Mango. She apologized for the delay."

"Mango hasn't been sent home yet?" Maybe the lizard was being held at customs.

"Of course not. She's still at the zoo. Isn't she?" Jason sounded confused.

"Not anymore. Officer Crosby from Border Force picked her up a couple of days ago. He said she was going home. I thought she would be there by now." Harriet had pictured the iguana basking in the Caribbean sunshine among her fellow creatures.

"That's weird. I don't know why he'd do that." Jason was silent for a moment. "I'll circle back around to my contact. Maybe they do have her."

"Let me know what you find out." Harriet was curious—and worried. Mango was extremely valuable. Had she somehow been lost in the shuffle?

"I will." Jason shifted the conversation to a lighter topic. "How's the zebra? I got your text."

"Are you sure you want to talk shop?" she teased. "He's fine. The cut is healing well." She thought of another bit of news. "I found a sand boa while walking the cliff trail."

A stunned silence fell. "Are you serious? Did it get away from someone?"

"We don't know. I met with a local reptile enthusiast, and he didn't know of any owners in the area. I'm concerned about two non-native reptiles showing up within a week."

"Did you inform Border Force?"

"Van Worthington, our local detective constable, said he would, and he's very reliable about such matters. He actually caught the snake." Harriet relayed the tale. "It's at the zoo right now. Apparently, that particular breed isn't a huge concern, meaning they won't ship him or her home."

"You're right. Sand boas are common pets. They don't belong loose here though."

Frustration gnawed at Harriet. When would they get answers? "Unless someone around here is very careless with their pets, I think there could be a smuggling problem in this area. Maybe smugglers have found a point of access. Officer Crosby said most animals come through the major airports. But this stretch of coastline has a history with smuggling, you know."

"It's very possible," Jason said. "Once I'm back at work, let's put our heads together about this, okay?"

"Sorry," Harriet said. "I didn't mean to intrude on your vacation."

"Not a problem. I called you, remember? But I don't have access to a lot of information right now."

"We'll talk soon then. Have a great rest of your time off."

"Thanks," Jason said. "My next ramble is the Standing Stones trail. You ever been out there? It's fantastic."

"Not yet. We're supposed to go this weekend." Harriet recalled Will mentioning the trail name when they'd firmed up the arrangements for Saturday.

"Maybe I'll see you out there. If not, have fun."

On the way home, Harriet realized she was near the address for Nick and Ozzie's business. She decided to take a quick detour and drive by the building.

This area of the village was mostly deserted at night, the narrow streets lined with metal and brick buildings used for commercial purposes. She found Nick's place, a long, low brick structure with a temporary sign by the office door, VOYAGER IMPORTS. It would be an import business rather than export, since the owners were now located in Yorkshire.

Her curiosity satisfied, Harriet drove on. She was almost back to the main road when a van with blue-and-black checks pulled into the lane. Border Force, with Officer Crosby at the wheel. Harriet honked her horn and flashed her lights.

The van slowed to a halt beside her, and she rolled down her window. The officer did the same.

"Hi, Officer Crosby. I've been wanting to catch up with you."

His expression remained stoic. "What can I do for you?"

"Mango, the rock iguana you picked up from Langford Hall. Where is she?"

His brow furrowed. "I'm not sure what you mean."

"My friend called the Wildlife Crimes Unit. They said they didn't have her."

He sighed, fingers tapping on the wheel. "The left hand doesn't know what the right hand is doing, I guess. I turned her in." He twisted in his seat as if searching on the passenger side. "Got the paperwork here. Somewhere."

"I believe you," Harriet said, not wanting him to bother. They were parked in the middle of the road, and another vehicle had pulled up behind her, waiting to proceed. "If you do hear that she's flown home, let me know, okay? I got kind of attached to her, so I'd like to know for sure that she's okay."

The car behind her honked, so Harriet didn't wait for his response. She rolled up her window and drove on. As she did, she murmured a prayer that Mango wasn't lost in transit.

Or stolen again.

CHAPTER EIGHTEEN

The hiking party set off at noon on Saturday. Harriet was at the wheel of the Land Rover, the roomiest choice for a day trip. Once the vet supplies and equipment were removed from the rear seat and cargo area anyway.

Polly sat in the front passenger seat, and Will and Van were in the back. They all wore hiking boots, jeans, wicking tops, fleece jackets, and windbreakers. Hats and gloves were a must as well, as were the slickers in their backpacks.

"I hope we don't get rain," Harriet said, eyeing the blue sky, which held a few fluffy clouds.

"We're not supposed to," Polly noted, checking the weather on her phone. "It's the moors, though. Bad weather can blow in anytime."

As they took the scenic route to the trailhead, Harriet relaxed against her seat with a sigh of contentment. She meant to savor every minute of this adventure. Will and Van were chatting, with Polly occasionally throwing in a remark. They all laughed at something, which warmed Harriet's heart. She was hopeful that Van and Polly would get back together, but in the meantime, she was glad they could all hang out as friends.

The road was winding and steep, with vistas of patchwork countryside in every direction. Now and then they passed by a farm, herds of cows and flocks of sheep grazing behind stone walls.

As they drew closer to the trail, Will directed Harriet. They passed through a small village and found the car park. Only a few other vehicles were in the lot.

"The hiking season hasn't really started yet," Will said. "In the summer, you have to fight for a parking space here. I usually arrive early in the morning."

Harriet was glad they'd found a spot so easily, since it was already midday. They donned their packs, made sure they had everything, and set off for the trail.

Right at the entrance stood a noticeboard with information about the park. "'The North York Moors contains one of the largest continuous areas of heather moorland in England,'" Harriet read. "'Special protection area for merlin and golden plover.'"

This was a new landscape for Harriet, and she was excited to explore it. The beginning of the trail was a beaten dirt path, and they gradually ascended through a grassy field. Ahead, they could see the trail winding over hills and dipping into valleys.

"This is beautiful," Harriet said. They ambled along at a relaxed pace, which she appreciated. In the past, she'd hiked with companions who were intent on racing to the top. Here there was only the countryside unfurling in front of them.

"Look," Polly said, pointing. A brown rabbit hopped across the grass toward the shelter of trees.

"As long as it's not an exotic bunny," Harriet joked. "Those aren't smuggled, are they?"

Snake in the Grass

"Don't think so." Van chuckled. "There's a fox."

Harriet had her binoculars around her neck, and she peered through them as the fox darted over the field. "He's healthy. Coat is nice and shiny."

"You would check the health of a wild animal," Polly teased her.

After about an hour of walking, they came across a stone wall that enclosed an abandoned farmhouse and barnyard. From there, they had a view across the moors, with Highland cattle grazing nearby.

"They've let the house remain standing for the wildlife," Will explained. "Birds and bats nest inside."

"Foxes too, apparently," Harriet said as another ran out of a low opening.

"Why don't we stop for lunch here?" Will suggested, taking off his pack. "We can sit in a sheltered spot next to the wall."

"Sounds good," Van said, and the women agreed.

They'd each brought something to share—sandwiches, crisps, fruit, and cookies. Van had a thermos of tea, and they each had water as well.

Harriet bit into a roast beef sandwich, savoring the taste. "I'm starving." Exercising outside certainly worked up an appetite.

"The next section is uphill," Will said. "There are standing stones at the top, plus some even more amazing views."

"You mentioned the stones," Harriet said. "I'm excited to see them." Yorkshire was home to quite a few standing stones, structures so ancient that people had forgotten why they were there.

"The sun feels so nice." Polly leaned back against the wall and closed her eyes.

"It's nice to have a day off," Van said, stealing a covert glance at Polly. "Been busier than ever."

Polly cracked open an eye. "Snake catching?" She grinned.

Van returned the smile. "Not lately."

"Speaking of snakes," Harriet chimed in, "Van, did you call Border Force about the snake we found? I forgot to ask Officer Crosby when I ran into him."

"When was that, Harriet?" Polly asked.

"The other night, when I went to check out Nick and Ozzie's company location. I saw his van and stopped to ask him about Mango."

"What's going on with Mango?" Van asked. "And yes, I did report the snake to Crosby. He hasn't gotten back to me on it yet."

Anxiety clenched in Harriet's belly at the thought of the iguana, and she regretted bringing up the subject. They were supposed to be taking a break today.

"Officer Crosby picked Mango up from Moorland Zoo," she explained. "He says he handed her over to the Wildlife Crimes Unit. But they told my colleague, Dr. Jason Peel, that they hadn't seen her."

Will frowned. "I don't like the sound of that. She's missing?"

"I hope not," Harriet said. "Officer Crosby said he has paperwork on her, but I didn't get a chance to see it. We were blocking traffic and someone honked at me, so I had to keep moving."

"I can check in with him," Van said. "We're the first line of contact in wildlife cases, so it's within my purview."

"Would you?" Harriet was relieved. No doubt the man would be more responsive to a fellow law enforcement officer. She had no standing except as a nosy civilian.

Van pulled out his phone. "Making a note right now."

"Are we ready to move on?" Will asked.

They gathered the remains of lunch, packed them, and set off again. As Will had said, the landscape grew steeper, the trail switch-backing along the hillside to compensate. Frequent stops to rest and take in the view enabled the party to make steady if slow progress.

"Hiking in New England is so different," Harriet said during one stop. "You're in the woods most of the time. The only open areas are on the mountain peaks, above the tree canopy." Now that they were up high, she could see across the valley to the trail on the other side, which they would take to return.

"We'll be in the woods part of the way." Will pointed out the route. "We descend and cross over a lane that leads past several farms. They own the cattle and sheep we've been seeing."

They weren't as remote as Harriet had thought. That was good to know.

"One last push," Van said. "I can see the stones up ahead."

They climbed up and over the last ridge to the lookout point. As promised, a stand of several stones kept watch over the valley. The chunks of granite were the height of a man and roughly cut. Up here, the wind was incessant, and Harriet could hear it whistling through the stones.

"It's both beautiful and eerie," she said, standing next to Will. From that spot, they could gaze out over miles of rolling moors in every direction. How many people had stood in this very place over the past millennia, admiring the view and listening to the wind whistle?

"Certainly puts things into perspective," Will said. "How tiny we are in the scope of things. Our lives are both short and eternal."

Harriet was comforted by the idea of eternity. It meant that people weren't truly lost, that she'd see them again someday. Her grandfather was right at the top of the list.

Scanning the valley below, she noticed a small stone structure tucked among overgrown bushes. "What's that?"

"It's an old crofter's hut. The trail will take us right past there."

Harriet used her binoculars to examine their surroundings. Something white on the ground behind some bushes caught her eye. Probably trash left by other hikers. They could pick it up when they got down there.

They wandered around near the stones for a while, taking in the sights in every direction. Harriet noticed that Van and Polly were chatting, so she left them alone and stayed with Will. They were standing near the stones when Will pulled a small notebook out of his jacket pocket and wrote in it.

"What are you writing?" Harriet asked.

"Sermon ideas. I often get inspired when I'm out walking or gardening. Even washing the dishes. Almost as if preaching should speak to real-life experiences or something." He grinned at her.

"Will I recognize this outing when I listen tomorrow?" Harriet asked, smiling.

"Perhaps." He tucked the notebook away and glanced at the sky. "We should probably get going. It'll take a couple of hours to get back to the trailhead."

They shouldered their packs again and set off along the trail.

The route went down, quite steeply in some spots. Harriet was careful where she placed her feet so she wouldn't slide on loose pebbles or soil. At one point, Polly did slip, but Van was right there to break her fall.

"I see you catch more than snakes," Polly joked. "Thanks for the help."

He waited until she was steady before releasing her arm. "Anytime, ma'am." They shared a laugh and continued on.

Harriet exchanged a smile with Will.

At the bottom of the slope, they traversed the valley, the fields green with new growth. The hills provided shelter from the wind, and the sun was warm enough that they took off their jackets and tied them around their waists.

As Will had said, the trail traveled right past the crofter's hut. Although the small building had an abandoned air, Harriet noticed that shutters were secured over the windows to keep the rain out.

"Interesting," Will said when he tried the door. "It's locked. This hut has always been open in case ramblers need shelter. No one has lived here for decades."

"Too bad we can't go in." Harriet had wanted to explore.

Polly took off her pack and opened it. "Anyone want a biscuit? I need energy for the climb back up the ridge."

While the others shared a snack break, Harriet wandered over to where she'd seen the flash of white from the standing stones. If a lot of hikers came through, it was no wonder there was litter left behind. So far, the trail had been surprisingly free of debris, but she supposed something might have been dropped and blown away from whoever brought it onto the trail.

She parted the bushes—and let out a shout of surprise.

Jason Peel lay sprawled on the ground, his eyes closed.

CHAPTER NINETEEN

"Jason!" Harriet cried, rushing to his side. Had he fallen and hit his head? It was his white sneakers that she'd seen, not a piece of trash. Harriet crouched beside him. With one hand, she took his pulse while with the other, she gingerly examined his head. He had a strong pulse—and a definite bump on the back of his head.

He should get medical attention immediately. Fortunately, her friends had already joined her, likely drawn by her shouts.

"What's going on?" Will asked. "Are you okay?"

"I am. He's not so good." Harriet gestured to Jason's prone form. "It's so strange. Jason told me he was doing this trail soon, but I never imagined we'd run into him like this." She'd pictured friendly greetings and a chat on the trail if they happened to see him.

Van crouched to examine Jason for himself, having first-response training.

"He's got a nasty bump on his head." Harriet pointed it out.

A groan brought Harriet's attention back to the stricken vet. His eyelids fluttered as he stirred.

"Jason, it's Harriet. Stay still. You hit your head." To the others, she added, "We need to get him to the hospital." It was a difficult prospect, being so far out on the trail.

Van retrieved his phone. "I'll call for an ambulance to meet me at the closest farm. I'll show them the way from there."

"They can use the lane I was talking about," Will said. "It's right over there, about fifty yards away."

Harriet pictured the medics with their gurney. "Not too far to carry him then."

Van frowned at his phone. "Not the best signal. I'd better start walking."

"I'll go with you," Polly offered.

"Good idea to stay in pairs," Will said.

"Text us an update," Harriet called as Van and Polly set off. "Hopefully, it will get through."

"Harriet?" Jason asked, his voice hoarse.

She sat beside him, glad to see his eyes were open and he was no longer trying to sit up. "What happened? Do you remember?"

His brow furrowed as he put a hand to his head. "I'm not sure. I heard a sheep bleating in the bushes. I thought it might be injured, so I went to investigate. That's all I remember."

"So you don't recall falling? Maybe tripping over this log?" Will nudged it with his foot.

"I don't remember anything." Jason closed his eyes. "Honestly."

Harriet's problem with Will's theory was that the injury was on the back of Jason's head. If he'd tripped and fallen, he most likely would have toppled forward and hit his forehead.

Harriet scanned the small clearing, studying the grass and ferns surrounded by bracken. No sign of a sheep—or any other creature, for that matter.

She noticed Will staring at the ground and went to join him. "What is it?"

He pointed to a shoe print in the mud.

Harriet eyed the pattern then compared it to Jason's sneaker. "It's not his." She put her foot next to it for comparison, careful not to damage the print. "It's bigger than mine, probably by at least three sizes." She pulled out her phone and took pictures. "We'd better show this to Van."

"You think someone hit him on the head?" Will asked in a low voice.

"Maybe." She explained her thoughts about the location of the injury. "He was face up when I found him, so maybe the attacker rolled him over."

Will rubbed the back of his neck. "Say someone hit him. But why? To rob him?"

"I can't see muggers lurking up here."

"Neither can I. It's not as if hikers usually carry a lot of valuables," Will mused. "And speaking of carrying, where is his pack? I assume he had one."

Harriet returned to Jason's side. "Let me check on him, and then we'll search for it." If a thief had been after his backpack, it was probably long gone.

Jason opened his eyes while Harriet hovered over him. "Can I sit up now?"

"No. We're waiting for an ambulance, so please, don't move." Harriet checked his pulse. Still steady. "Did you have a backpack?"

"Yes. It's red. Should be near the trail."

"We'll see if we can find it. You stay put." Harriet joined Will once more. "We didn't see it, so maybe he came from the other direction."

They hurried along the trail, keeping their eyes peeled for the rucksack. They found it nestled in the grass at the foot of a tree.

Will picked up the pack and peered inside the main compartment. "Rain jacket. An empty paper bag. Water bottle." He unzipped the front. "Wallet and keys."

Harriet rested her hands on her hips. "So he probably wasn't robbed. The person who hit him might not have seen the pack."

"You mean they were after Jason himself?" Will's blunt question sent a chill down Harriet's spine.

"I don't know what to think. I don't get it." Harriet surveyed the area, the crofter's hut, the path leading through the valley. "Did he encounter trouble—or bring it with him? I must admit, I don't know much about Jason beyond our few conversations."

"Good question," Will said, his gaze somber. "Unless there's someone randomly targeting ramblers."

"I sure hope not." Harriet winced at the idea. "Still, a warning better go out not to hike alone." Her phone chimed, and she read the text. "Van and Polly made it to the farm and called an ambulance. Should be here in twenty minutes or so."

Harriet kept vigil over Jason while Will continued to scour the area. They'd marked the shoe impression with upright sticks so no one would step on it and ruin the print.

Eventually, Harriet heard the rumble of a vehicle engine in the distance. "They're coming," she told Jason, patting his shoulder. While waiting, she'd confirmed that he had been hiking alone. The red pack was at his side, ready to be taken with him to the hospital.

Soon the EMTs pushed through the bushes, carrying a gurney and led by Polly and Van.

While the medics worked to check Jason and prepare him for transport, Will and Harriet shared what they'd learned. They also showed Van the footprint.

"You think it belonged to the assailant?" Van asked.

"Maybe." Harriet shrugged. "The location of the injury indicates to me that he was struck. If he'd fallen forward, as is more likely if he'd tripped, he'd probably have hit the front or side of his head."

Van took that in, nodding. "I'm tagging along with him to the hospital. Maybe he'll remember more details as he recovers. Otherwise, I'll be opening a case."

The medics had Jason secured and were ready to start carrying him to the ambulance.

"What should we do?" Harriet asked. "I don't think we have time to finish the hike."

"The farmer said he'd be happy to take us back to the parking lot," Polly said.

"Let's go then," Will said.

After saying goodbye to Van and Jason, the trio started walking along the lane, which was rutted from past traffic. Still, it was flat and much easier than hiking the hills.

The ambulance rumbled past, requiring them to move over to the verge. "I hope Jason will be all right," Polly said, watching the ambulance recede into the distance.

"Me too." Harriet was thankful they had found Jason. They hadn't seen another hiker all day. There was no telling how long he might have lain there before he was found—or what might have happened to him in the meantime.

The bigger questions were who would hit Jason and why?

"Is there any illegal activity out here on the moors?" she asked Will. "I'm wondering what Jason ran into."

Will shrugged. "I don't know of anything specific, but it's isolated enough that criminals would be able to operate in secrecy."

"I wonder if the farmer knows anything," Harriet said. "Maybe he saw something. Or someone."

"Van asked him, and he said he hadn't," Polly replied. "He also told us he'd been in town most of the day."

As they rounded a corner, Harriet saw a farmhouse with outbuildings ahead. "Is that the place?"

To her surprise, Polly shook her head. "No one was there. It's the next farm."

As they passed the farm, Harriet studied the property. She saw a few sheep grazing in a pasture, but as Polly had said, no vehicles were in the yard.

A few minutes later, they came to another farm. Polly put on a burst of speed. "This is it." She led them down a short drive to the farmyard, where a burly man was unloading hay bales from a trailer. He waved when he saw them.

"You're back," he said to Polly. His eyes were keen, his smile tentative. "How'd it go with the injured hiker? Saw the ambulance."

"He should be okay," Polly said. "Mac, these are my friends, Pastor Will Knight and Dr. Harriet Bailey."

Mac gave Harriet an interested glance. "Doc Bailey's granddaughter? I've heard about you."

"I hope you've heard good things," Harriet said with a laugh. "Call me Harriet."

"Very complimentary indeed. I'm Mac Petch." He took off his gloves to shake hands. "You still need a ride to the trailhead?"

"We do," Polly said. "If you have time."

"Not a problem. I can take you in my truck." He gestured to a pickup with front and back seats. "Climb aboard."

"We really appreciate this," Harriet told him, taking off her pack. She had a few questions to ask Mac, so she was glad when her friends insisted that she sit up front.

"Excuse the mess," Mac said as he started the truck. "You know how it is."

Harriet took in the muddy floor mats, dog hair, assorted farm supplies, and pungent aroma of livestock with a smile. "Sure do." Her Land Rover was often in a similar condition, and Harriet wasn't one to critique the housekeeping—or, rather, truck-keeping—of someone who was helping her.

"I'm so glad we came along when we did," she said as they bumped along the lane to the main road. "My friend might have been lying there all night with no one the wiser."

Mac's glance was sharp. "You know him?"

"He's a vet specializing in exotic animals, so we've crossed paths," Harriet explained. "He had a head injury, and I don't think he could have walked out."

The farmer winced. "Head injury? Yikes. What happened?"

"We're not sure," Harriet said. "And he doesn't remember. Did you see anyone else on the lane today? We were hoping to find a witness." *And the assailant.*

"No, I didn't see anyone," Mac said. "I wasn't home for a good portion of the day though."

Harriet thought of another question. "Who owns the crofter's hut? Do you?"

Mac glanced both ways before pulling out on the main road. "On your way to my place, you passed Isaac Dinsdale's farm. He owns it. Way back, they used to have a shepherd live there while the sheep were grazing. Not anymore."

Maybe they should talk to the owner, although that was a stretch. Just because Jason was attacked near the hut didn't mean the incident was related to the building.

"He finally had to lock it up," Mac went on. "Board up the windows. Kids were going inside, setting fires, getting up to all kinds of mischief."

"That's too bad," Will said from the back seat. "It was a convenient shelter if hikers got caught in bad weather."

The farmer sighed. "That's the way it is these days. People don't respect private property. More than one person has tossed trash onto my land from the road."

"I don't understand littering," Harriet said with sympathy. "We're all responsible for this world we live in."

Mac snorted. "Evidently some people missed that memo. I picked up a whole bag of garbage today, as a matter of fact."

"How awful," Harriet said.

"I've told Isaac more than once that we should gate this road," Mac said. "Make it a little harder for people to get in here and cause trouble."

Or get up to mischief that results in a man getting hit in the head.

CHAPTER TWENTY

"Thank you so much," Harriet told Mac when he pulled up beside her vehicle. "You saved us hours of hiking."

"No problem," he said. "I hope that young man will be okay. Will you let me know?" He pointed to the side of his truck panel, which bore the name of his farm and a phone number.

Polly snapped a shot. "We'll do that, soon as we know anything."

With a wave, Mac drove away, leaving the trio standing near the Land Rover.

Harriet felt suddenly deflated as she dug for her keys. "Not the way I thought this day would end." She unlocked the doors then opened the back gate for the packs.

She recognized one of the few cars in the lot as Jason's. It hadn't been there when they arrived, so he must have taken the loop trail in the opposite direction. He hadn't passed them.

"What next?" Will asked. "Want to go to the hospital and check on Jason?"

Polly looked at her phone. "Van said they took him to the hospital in Whitby. By the time we get there, someone might have news."

They stowed their packs and headed out.

"The trail was really awesome," Harriet told Will, who was sitting in the passenger seat. Polly was in the back, busy on her phone.

"I can't wait to go hiking again—as long as we don't run into more trouble like this."

"I usually don't," Will said, his smile sympathetic. "I find these excursions refreshing. They allow me to get away from it all and spend time with God in the great outdoors."

"I know what you mean." During the outing, Harriet had felt as though all her worries were far away.

"What part of the trail did you like best?" Will asked.

"The stones were amazing with the view and the sense of history. I also liked being out on the moors, seeing the plants and the birds and the wildlife. So different from what I'm used to."

"I have a lot of other sites to show you." Will's smile was warm. "I enjoy sharing things with you, Harriet. It's like experiencing them myself for the first time."

"I'm so glad you feel that way. I'm having a wonderful time too." Harriet was thrilled at the idea of exploring her new homeland with Will. He was a warm, witty companion who made her feel truly seen and heard.

With Will's directions, Harriet easily found the hospital, a blocky structure located in the middle of Whitby. As she pulled into a visitor's space, she asked Polly, "Can you text Van and find out what's going on? I wonder if they'll let us see Jason. Probably not if he's in the emergency room, especially since we aren't family."

"Jason's having a head scan now," Polly said, reading from her phone. "He's fully conscious, so it doesn't look like he'll be admitted. They're just being thorough."

"Thank God," Will said fervently. "I'm so glad."

"Me too." Harriet tugged the keys from the ignition. "Want to get a cup of tea in the cafeteria and wait? If they do release Jason, he'll need a ride home." She hadn't planned on driving to York, but she'd happily do it to help a friend.

"That sounds good to me," Polly said. "Although, he'll need to get his car somehow."

"I saw it at the trailhead," Harriet said. "We can swing by there and pick it up."

Will opened his door. "We'll figure it out. Polly, will you let Van know we'll be in the cafeteria?"

"Will do." Polly sent a quick text and then climbed out of the vehicle.

The main café was closed, but they were able to buy to-go cups of tea from a kiosk. Instead of sitting in a waiting room, they carried their cups out to a bench in the garden. Every step of the way, Polly kept Van informed. Harriet was glad to see such consistent communication between the pair.

"This isn't the moors, but it is nice." Will tilted his face up to the sun. "Let's say a prayer for Jason." He led them in a prayer for healing for their friend, and that the truth of what had happened to him would be revealed.

Harriet and Polly gave a hearty amen when he finished. "I'm so thankful we have God to lean on," Harriet said. "Sometimes it's all far too much for me to handle."

"Isn't that the truth?" Polly straightened, her eyes sparkling. "Here comes Van."

The detective constable emerged from the hospital and veered in their direction.

"The head scan was normal," he announced. "He's going to be released to go home. Which raises the issue of transport."

"We've already discussed it," Will said. "We need to go to his car, and then we can tandem down to his place. He shouldn't drive."

"You and I can do it, Will," Van offered. To Harriet and Polly, he said, "You two can drop us off at my place."

"I don't mind driving either," Will said. "I get some great sermon ideas when I'm behind the wheel."

"I want to go," Polly said. "Make sure he's settled okay."

"So do I," Harriet said. "He shouldn't be alone tonight. Does he have a roommate? Or maybe family he can stay with?"

Van rubbed his chin. "I can't answer those questions. If he doesn't have anyone, other ideas?"

Will raised his hand. "He can bunk at the rectory. I don't mind nurse duty for a night."

"Even with church tomorrow?" Harriet asked.

"I'll be fine."

With the plan settled, Van went back inside to check on Jason. The others sat and talked until Van texted Polly that Jason was being released and had accepted Will's invitation to stay with him. Harriet drove the Land Rover around to the entrance.

Within a few minutes, Van pushed Jason out in a wheelchair, accompanied by a nurse.

Jason waved when he saw them waiting. His head was bandaged, but he was smiling. His backpack rested in his lap.

Van helped him into the front seat, and the nurse took the wheelchair away.

"Thanks so much, guys," Jason said as they set off. "I'm glad you came along when you did."

"Me too," Harriet said. "Next stop, the rectory. Then we'll go get your car and bring it back to White Church Bay."

"That's not necessary," Jason protested. "It's probably okay where it is. You're already doing too much for me."

"We don't mind," Harriet said. "Happy to help a friend."

With that settled, Jason lapsed into silence. When Harriet glanced at him, she saw that his eyes were closed. The poor guy. What an ordeal.

She shuddered to think how much worse it could have been. If he'd been hit harder or left outside overnight... She forced herself to stop thinking about it. Her nerves were already frayed.

Harriet pulled up in front of the rectory, which was located next door to the church. Will came around to help Jason out while Van carried the men's packs.

"We'll see you soon," Harriet called to Will and Jason. Van returned to the vehicle with Jason's keys, and they were off again.

"Do you want to go home, Polly?" Harriet asked. It would only be a short detour to drop her off.

"No, I want to go," Polly replied. "I have nothing else planned."

"I thought we could grab a cuppa to go for the ride if you've got enough petrol, Harriet," Van said.

"Great idea," Harriet agreed. "Let's do it."

After the scheduled stop, they headed back into the moors. They'd been riding for about twenty minutes when Van said, "Would you mind taking the right-hand turn that's coming up? I want to check around the crofter's hut again."

"Fine with me." Harriet wasn't averse to investigating. "What did Jason tell you?"

"Not much, unfortunately." Van put his to-go cup in the holder and opened his phone. "He said he stopped for lunch."

That fit with the bag and empty wrappers in his pack.

"After eating, he decided to explore. Thinking he heard voices, he went toward the hut. He didn't see anyone, so he figured they were far away. Sound carries, right? Then he heard the sound of a distressed sheep in the bushes. The next thing he knew, we were there and his head hurt."

"Someone didn't want him to see them," Harriet guessed. "But why?"

Van's jaw hardened. "Could be any number of things. The moors, being so isolated, are sometimes used for criminal activities."

Once they reached the lane, Harriet was glad for the Beast's sturdy suspension and clearance. Even so, she had to keep the speed to a crawl. As they passed Mac's farm, Harriet saw him on his tractor and gave him a wave. She'd already texted him about Jason's prognosis. "He probably wonders what we're doing back here."

"He'll find out soon enough when I question him," Van muttered. He leaned forward as the next farm came into view. "Still no one home. That's a shame."

At the end of the lane, Harriet pulled over to the side and parked. There wasn't an official parking lot there. Someone had tacked a sign on a post.

CARRY IN, CARRY OUT.
PASS AT YOUR OWN RISK.
DON'T FEED THE SHEEP OR CATTLE.

Following the packed trail, the trio made their way to the crofter's hut. The afternoon was quiet, broken only by the occasional cry of a bird.

"Tell us what to do," Polly said to Van. "We want to be helpful."

Van divided the area into sections, and they each took one to search.

Harriet walked with her head down, scanning the grass, bushes, and trees for any sign of human activity. She found none, and neither did Van or Polly.

"Too bad whoever was here seems to have obeyed the sign asking people to carry out whatever they brought in," Polly said.

Harriet groaned. "Just our luck, right? Conscientious criminals." Then she thought of something Mac had said. "Mac mentioned that he picked up a whole bag of garbage today. It might be a long shot, but—"

"But it's worth asking about," Van finished for her.

They returned to Mac's land, and Van went to meet the farmer on his tractor. After conferring for a moment, Mac nodded and drove across the field to his house.

"He still has the bag," Van said as he climbed back into the Land Rover. "He's going to let us examine it."

"He must have found it a strange request," Harriet said.

"Probably, but I told him the truth," Van said. "That we're investigating Jason's injury, and the bag might hold a clue as to who else was at the hut. We have to start somewhere."

"No stone left unturned, right?" Polly inserted brightly.

Van smiled at her. "Exactly."

Harriet drove into the farmyard again, and the farmer joined them there a few minutes later.

Mac cut the tractor engine and swung himself off the machine. "It's in the shed, with the other trash. I lock it up to keep animals out." A black-and-white collie mix loped across the yard to greet his master. "Like you, Jed. He's the worst offender."

Harriet bent to rub the dog's ears. "I bet you are. But you're a good boy, aren't you?" Jed panted happily. As Mac led them to the shed, Jed introduced himself to Polly and Van as well. Then he glued himself to his master's heels.

"He knows what I'm doing," Mac said. He pulled out a set of keys and unlocked the padlock securing the door. Several barrels and bins for recycling stood inside the shed. Mac opened a barrel to extract a black garbage bag. "Here you go. Is there anything else I can help you with?"

Van considered. "If you happen to see unfamiliar vehicle traffic going by over the next couple of days, please make a note."

"You mean make, model, plate?" Mac sounded excited by the idea.

"As many details as possible. Oh, and if you see any more litter, pick it up and save it, will you?"

Mac hovered. "Are you taking the bag with you?"

"We'll take a quick look, and if it's not of any use, we'll return it to the shed and secure the padlock."

"Good enough," Mac said. "I'd better get back to work."

Van gave him a wave. "We appreciate your help." He reached into his pocket and pulled out a pair of disposable gloves. At Harriet's and Polly's questioning looks, he said, "Got these from the EMTs. I don't carry them everywhere I go."

Jed nosed in to investigate when Van untied the bag.

Harriet grabbed the dog's collar and gently tugged him away. Polly picked up a stray stick and tossed it. Jed bolted to fetch it.

"Brilliant, Polly." Van opened the bag a little more.

Harriet braced herself for bad odors. But instead of the expected food waste, she saw several plastic containers and packets. Empty water jugs too.

Van reached into the bag and grabbed the first container, which had a colorful label. "Iguana food. How many people carry that on a hike?"

The answer to that was zero. There was no reason to have iguana food unless one had an iguana.

Like, say, Mango, whose whereabouts were currently unaccounted for.

CHAPTER TWENTY-ONE

"Iguana food?" Polly echoed. "How strange."

Van was sorting through the containers in the bag. "Most of them used to contain reptile food. There are also a few crisp and candy bags. And water bottles."

"Reptiles need water," Polly pointed out.

Harriet nodded. "True." She pictured someone filling water dishes from the empty gallon jugs. "Maybe someone at the Dinsdale farm keeps reptiles. Or one of the kids who was up here."

"Both are possibilities," Van said. "But in light of Jason being attacked, the crofter's hut interests me. Though I know it's a stretch to think that incident is related to this." He shook the bag slightly.

"You know, when I took care of Mango, I gave her fresh food," Harriet said. "Vets recommend that no more than five to ten percent of their diet should be pellets or canned."

"No scraps of vegetables or fruit in here," Van said, further cementing Harriet's theory.

Harriet pointed at the bag. "Those containers speak to convenience, not prioritizing quality animal care."

"What are you saying?" Van asked.

"That the trash didn't come from a pet owner," Harriet said. Someone who viewed the creatures as a commodity might not be fussy about their diet."

Polly jumped in. "I agree. I didn't see any pellets at Eddie's."

"Eddie?" Van asked. Perhaps it was wishful thinking on Harriet's part, but she thought she detected a note of jealousy in his voice.

"Reptile owner in White Church Bay," Polly explained. "My brother's friend. We visited him to see if he knew anything about smugglers in the area. He invited us to a meeting of reptile owners next week."

Van nodded in approval. "Smart. I should've thought of that."

Polly waved her hand. "We were going to fill you in if we learned anything."

The detective constable returned his gaze to the bag. "I'm going to take this into evidence. Before we head out, I need to confirm with Mac when and where he found it."

"That's fine," Harriet said. "We'll hang out with Jed while you do that. Do you mind if I take a couple of pictures for my own reference?"

Van nodded at the Land Rover. "Why don't we put the bag in the boot, and you can take your pictures there? I'll pull out some of the containers for you."

"Great, thank you." Van's offer spoke to the relationship Harriet had built with the officer. He trusted her to be of help in solving a case, not a hindrance.

Harriet opened the back of the vehicle, and Van arranged the items for her to photograph. Then he returned them all to the bag. "I'm going to go talk to Mac. See you in a few." He strode off toward the field, Jed at his heels.

Polly pointed to the bag. "This could be a real breakthrough. Maybe the smugglers are keeping some reptiles out here somewhere."

"It's possible." Although Harriet was equally encouraged, she was trying not to leap to conclusions. "Maybe Van can get fingerprints off the containers."

"I bet he will." Polly sounded certain. "He's really good at his job."

Harriet bit back a smile. "Yes, he is." She pulled out her phone. "I'm going to give Will an update. He might be wondering what's keeping us." She sent a text and was delighted to receive a reply within moments. "Will says Jason is resting and feeling better every minute."

"I'm so relieved. I can't believe someone did such an awful thing." Polly watched Van make his way back through the field toward them. "We need to catch whoever it was."

"Totally agree." Harriet's energy was flagging now. "I can't wait to take a hot shower and curl up with a book. What a day."

"It's been a roller coaster, for sure." Polly brightened. "I have an idea. Why don't we get pizza tonight? The four of—oh, Will might want to stay with Jason."

"We'll take it to the rectory." Harriet sent Will another text. "We never did get the post-hike pub meal Will mentioned." They had planned to stop on their way home to enjoy a nice dinner.

"You won't believe it," Van said when he was within earshot. "Guess when Mac found the trash?"

"Around the time Jason was attacked?" Harriet guessed.

"Bingo," Van said. "Mac found it right before the ambulance arrived. It wasn't there earlier."

"Fits the timeline then." Harriet was pleased. Although not conclusive, the timing of the discard was telling. "I wish he'd spotted whoever tossed it."

"Me too," Van said with a sigh. "Let's go pick up Jason's car."

"Want pizza for dinner?" Polly asked. "Harriet and I are taking some over to Will's."

"Sounds good." Van opened the front passenger door. "You take the front, Polly. I'm going to be working on my notes." After shutting the door behind her, he climbed into the back.

Harriet got behind the wheel, and they set off on the next leg of their adventure.

"This is really hitting the spot," Will said before taking another bite of pepperoni pizza. "So glad you suggested it, Polly."

"Me too." Harriet took another slice of veggie pizza, which featured a wide variety of vegetables, all the perfect tenderness.

"Thanks for fetching my car," Jason said. Although he still wore a rather rakish bandage, the color had returned to his cheeks. "Saves me a bunch of hassle."

"Not a problem," Van said. "We did come across something interesting when we went back to Mac's farm." Jason had been napping when they'd first arrived, so they hadn't told him about the bag of trash.

Seeing Jason's puzzled expression, Harriet clarified. "Mac Petch owns one of the farms on the dirt road leading to the croft. He gave us a ride back to my car this afternoon."

Jason stabbed at his salad with a fork. "Any clues as to who hit me?"

"Maybe." Van selected another slice of pizza. "Harriet, can you show him the pictures?"

After wiping her hands, Harriet brought up the photos on her phone. "Mac found a bag of trash on his land around the same time you were hurt. This is what was inside."

Jason studied the pictures. "Reptile food? That's strange."

"It really is," Will commented. "I've seen all kinds of trash on the trail, but that's a new one on me."

Jason glanced up sharply. "You think someone's been using the hut to keep reptiles?" He'd quickly made the leap to the same conclusion Harriet had.

"It's possible," Van said slowly. "I need to get in there and see. Already placed a call to the property owner. If he's not cooperative, I'll ask the judge for a search warrant."

Polly clapped. "Way to go, Van."

Van ducked his head, the tips of his ears flushing bright pink. "It was the next logical step. We could be totally wrong. The fact remains, though, that someone was threatened by your presence, Jason."

"Because of his profession, you think?" Harriet asked. "He might notice things other people would miss."

"It's possible," Van acknowledged. "Or they didn't want anyone snooping around who might be able to identify them later."

"Can I go with you?" Jason asked. "If you find reptiles, you'll need me to evaluate them. If they're gone, I might be able to identify evidence of their presence."

"I'd love to go along as well," Harriet said. If reptiles were being held captive in a windowless hut, she wanted to help them. "If they're keeping reptiles there, they need heat and light. I wonder if the power is connected."

Van took out his phone and tapped at the screen several times. Harriet realized he was searching some kind of database when he said, "Yes, there is power available at the hut. I'll need to either ask the owner or contact the utility company to find out if it's an active account."

"I think we're on the verge of a breakthrough," Harriet said. "I can feel it."

When Harriet walked into church the next morning, she was pleased to see Victoria Langford seated beside Jason Peel. She would have joined them, but the seats around them were taken. Aunt Jinny was out of town, visiting a friend. So Harriet contented herself by sitting near the back, where she could intercept Victoria and Jason when they left.

Will's sermon was on Luke 8:17. He opened his Bible and read, "'For there is nothing hidden that will not be disclosed, and nothing concealed that will not be known or brought out into the open.'" Harriet recalled his prayer focused on that very thought, that the truth would be revealed.

"This passage can be intimidating," Will said. "We all have things we try to hide, don't we?" The congregation chuckled ruefully. "We even try to hide them from God. We want to present our best selves to Him, so we keep the shameful parts hidden. But that's not how an honest relationship with Him works. It can be a comfort to confess all to God, since He knows it anyway."

Harriet reflected as he spoke, applying the lesson to herself. *Search me, God, and know my heart.* It was comforting to realize that He loved her despite her faults and failures.

She also hoped the verse would apply to other situations, such as what had really happened on the sailboat before it sank. And the possible reptile smuggling.

That thought led her to wonder once again, where was Mango? Could she be in the hut? Or had she been at one point? Harriet prayed they would find her and be able to send her home.

Harriet lingered in her row after the service, edging out to join Jason and Victoria when they reached her. "Hi," she said to Jason. "How are you feeling?" He wore a smaller bandage today, and Victoria was lovely in a floral cotton dress and a cardigan.

"I'm doing well, thank you," he said. "Will insists that I stay another night before I make the drive home."

"I agree with him," Victoria chimed in. "What a shocking thing to happen." Her features creased with concern when she glanced at his bandage.

"Want to come over for lunch?" Harriet asked. "It won't be fancy. Sandwiches and soup."

"That sounds perfect to me," Victoria said. "I have employees to cover the zoo for the couple of hours we're open this afternoon. It'll be fine, as long as I get there before closing."

When they reached Will, who was greeting parishioners, Harriet invited him to lunch as well. "Victoria and Jason are coming. Hopefully Polly and Van too."

"I'd be happy to," Will said, squeezing Harriet's hand. "Should I bring orange squash? I have plenty." The sweet orange drink was perfect for a spring lunch outdoors.

Harriet beamed at him. "Perfect. See you at noon."

Back at home, Harriet greeted Maxwell and Charlie, changed into jeans and a T-shirt, and then began to rustle up lunch. She had most of a roast chicken, which she decided to turn into chicken salad using her grandmother's recipe of mayonnaise, curry powder, golden raisins, chutney, celery, and lemon juice.

Polly rapped on the back door, left open to the warm day. "Knock, knock. Special delivery." She carried a cheerful cookie tin.

"Let me guess. Doreen Danby."

"She hailed me as I was going by." Polly set the tin on the table and opened it. "Strawberry tarts. Yum."

"Doreen is amazing." Harriet set the chicken on a cutting board and began to trim it. "Can you check the pantry for tomato soup?"

"Sure thing." Polly popped into the pantry and soon returned with the soup. "I'll get this started."

"Thanks." As she prepared the sandwich filling, Harriet reflected on the remaining tasks. They could serve themselves in the kitchen and then take their food out to the table, which held six at a pinch. Which reminded her of Van.

"Do you care if Van joins us?" Harriet asked Polly.

"Not at all." Polly was opening the cans of soup. "It's getting easier and easier to be around him."

"I'm glad to hear it." Harriet held up her hands. "Do you mind texting him? My hands have chicken all over them."

Polly chuckled. "No problem." She sent the text and then returned to warming the soup. Her phone bleeped with a notification. "He's coming."

"Great. There's plenty of chicken salad." Harriet mixed the spices and chutney with the mayonnaise before adding it to the bowl of chicken, along with diced celery and raisins. Savory with a touch of sweetness. Grandma Helen's recipe never missed.

The guests arrived at the same time in a burst of laughter and chatter. Harriet was thrilled to welcome such a good group of friends to her home. She joined the banter as she set out what they would need. "Help yourselves, everyone. We're going to eat in the garden."

They settled around the table, still chattering away. "This is lovely," Victoria said, gazing around. Then she glanced down at Maxwell next to her feet. "So's he."

"Don't feed him," Harriet warned. "He gets plenty of treats."

Charlie was hanging out too, seated on the stone wall in the sun to keep an eye on the proceedings. Harriet had already sneaked a tiny piece of chicken breast to her. The cat adored chicken.

Van's phone rang while they were clearing the table for dessert. "Excuse me. I need to take this." He got up and wandered away. "Good news," he said a few minutes later when he returned. "Isaac Dinsdale is willing to let me into the hut."

CHAPTER TWENTY-TWO

Van arranged the meeting for three, which gave the group plenty of time to finish lunch and relax before setting out again.

"Do you think the attack on Jason had something to do with the reptile smuggling?" Victoria asked.

"Maybe," Harriet said. "It's all a theory right now, based on finding the bag of reptile food containers. But we might not find anything inside the hut. Remember how Officer Crosby picked Mango up from the zoo?"

"How could I forget?" Victoria replied. "He was rather unpleasant about it."

Harriet nodded in agreement. "Apparently, no one from the Wildlife Crimes Unit has seen her. And when I ran into him, he said he'd turned her in."

"Slipped between the cracks," Van said, skepticism heavy in his voice. "An iguana worth tens of thousands of pounds."

"Wow, that's awful," Victoria said. "So either someone stole her again or—"

"She was never turned in." Van raised a hand. "I'm not accusing anyone, mind. It's definitely suspicious though."

Harriet prayed that wherever Mango was she was being treated well. Hopefully the person wouldn't be so careless as to let her escape into the chilly English countryside again.

Van glanced at his phone. "We'd better get ready to head out. I'm going to take the official vehicle. Can you follow me, Harriet?"

"Sure thing. And Jason can ride with me."

"I guess I'll head home," Victoria said. "It was nice to see you all." The group echoed the sentiment.

"I'll walk you out." Harriet wanted an opportunity to catch up with Victoria in private. She hadn't seen her since Victoria had discovered the missing giraffe statue at Langford Hall.

They paused beside Victoria's vehicle to talk. "Thanks again for inviting me," she said. "It's nice to just hang out and forget about my troubles once in a while."

"I hear you." In light of Victoria's words, Harriet thought better of her plan to ask for an update. Instead she said, "You and Jason seemed to be getting along well."

Victoria smiled. "Yes. Things are going swimmingly. We're going out to dinner next week."

"That's great." Harriet was always delighted when one of her friends found a special someone. "Maybe we can all get together again sometime soon."

"I'd like that. On another note, there's nothing new with Nick. He's barely ever home now that they've moved the business. I think he's staying with Ozzie somewhere."

"I'm sorry, Victoria." Harriet fully sympathized. "It's such a difficult situation."

"It is." Victoria's expression hardened. "As much as I love my brother, I have to keep the welfare of the zoo foremost in my mind. If it's closed down, who knows where the animals would end up? They're my responsibility."

Harriet couldn't argue with that.

Victoria opened her handbag and pulled out a set of keys. "I'd better get back. Check on the zoo."

"It was good to see you," Harriet said. "Stay in touch."

"You too. Especially if you find Mango." Victoria's eyes flashed. "Or my missing genet. I have no idea where she went. I've noticed an awful lot of missing things around Langford Hall these days."

Harriet had almost forgotten about the genet. She watched as Victoria started her vehicle and backed out of the parking space. With a final wave, she returned to the house. Time to get ready for the next adventure.

"How are you feeling?" Harriet asked Jason, who was in the passenger seat of the Land Rover. Then she cringed. "Sorry. I know people keep asking you that."

He laughed. "It's okay. I'm glad people care." He touched the bandage lightly. "I'm almost back to normal. Whatever that is for me." He grinned.

Harriet laughed. "I'm glad. I'm also glad that you're hanging around White Church Bay for a couple of days. Can I ask you a few questions?"

"Sure. Fire at will." Jason settled back, his expression attentive.

For the rest of the drive to the farm behind Van in the police car, the two vets chatted about exotic animal care. Harriet was happy for the opportunity to learn, to broaden her knowledge base and be able to serve more animals well.

"Polly introduced me to a friend of hers who keeps reptiles," she told him. "We're going to attend a meeting of enthusiasts tomorrow night, and it's possible some might become clinic clients."

"If you ever need advice, contact me," Jason said. "Or one of my colleagues. But I'm confident you can handle most of the issues you'll run into."

"I hope so." Harriet wanted to be prepared if she was asked to treat a snake or other reptile. Maybe keeping such creatures as pets wasn't to her taste, but she'd seen the fondness in Eddie's eyes. "I met a chameleon the other day. What a cool animal."

"They truly are." Jason shared several experiences he'd had with rare species of reptiles. "I have to admit, though, Mango is my favorite."

"Mine too," Harriet said. "I hope we find her."

They bumped along the now-familiar lane, following Van past Mac's farm and to the Dinsdale place. A truck sat next to the barn, and as the two vehicles pulled up, a burly farmer emerged. He stood watching their approach, feet braced and thumbs hooked in his suspenders.

"Mr. Isaac Dinsdale?" Van inquired. "I'm DC Worthington with the White Church Bay police. These are my veterinary consultants, Dr. Harriet Bailey and Dr. Jason Peel."

Harriet and Jason murmured greetings.

Mr. Dinsdale regarded them with a gimlet eye. "What do you need vets for? I thought you were going to poke around inside the crofter's hut."

"We think someone might have been keeping animals inside the building," Van explained.

Mr. Dinsdale rocked back on his heels. "Animals? What kind of animals?"

"We found reptile food containers on another farmer's land," Van said.

The farmer pursed his lips. "My nephew didn't mention keeping reptiles there. I'm not happy about that. The place doesn't have running water right now."

Van leaped in eagerly. "Your nephew was using the place? What's his name?"

"Craig Dinsdale," Mr. Dinsdale said. "He had a key. That's all. I'm not saying he did anything, understand?"

"I do," Van assured him. "We appreciate you letting us check it out."

Mr. Dinsdale pulled a ring of keys out of his pocket and began flipping through them. "Make sure you lock up after yourselves. I've had a lot of trouble with kids making messes in there."

"You don't want to go with us?" Van asked.

The farmer handed over the key. "Nah. Cows need milking."

Van shifted on his feet, frowning. "All right. If we do find anything of interest, I'll call you. I want the whole process to be transparent."

Mr. Dinsdale adjusted his cap. "Fair enough. I doubt you'll find anything. The place was swept clean last time I checked."

"Which was?"

"Oh, a month or two ago. I peek in there every now and then."

Tucking the key into a shirt pocket and buttoning it, Van said, "Thanks for your cooperation. We'll be back shortly. Or I will be calling you."

They drove to the end of the road and parked. They followed the path to the crofter's hut, Van carrying an evidence kit and Harriet toting her medical bag.

The scene was peaceful, with puffy clouds chasing one another across a blue sky. Birds called and sang, and the sunshine was warm.

"It's hard to believe someone attacked me here," Jason said, staring toward the stand of trees where Harriet had found him.

"Are you okay?" she asked, realizing belatedly that he might have a traumatic reaction to visiting the site so soon.

Shaking himself, he tore his gaze from the trees. "Yeah, I'm fine. I hope we catch whoever hit me."

"So do I," Van said as he unlocked the padlock on the door. He pulled a flashlight from his duty belt and switched it on, aiming the beam into the space. He went in, and a light flickered on. "Power's connected."

Harriet opened her bag and passed out gloves. All three put them on.

"Something was definitely kept here," Jason said, pausing inside the doorway and sniffing.

"Yep." Harriet smelled it too—wood bark and coconut fibers. Materials that were used for reptile bedding.

"Can we enter smells into evidence?" Jason joked.

"Not with present-day technology." Van was pacing around the place, which held minimal furnishings. A rustic table and chairs.

An old peat-burning stove and a deep sink. The lone bulb above them was dim, so he used his flashlight to search the corners.

Suddenly, he got down on his knees and reached for something under the sink, which was enclosed with a faded calico curtain.

Harriet and Jason hurried over, eager to view the find. It was a fragment of paper from the top of a food pouch. Part of the label was visible.

"I recognize that brand," Jason said. "It's a company that makes packaged reptile snacks." He retrieved his phone, frowning as he checked for a signal. "Ah. Here we go." He tapped on the screen then showed them a website featuring the packets.

"This could be a connection between this hut and the trash we found," Van said. "Maybe the rest of the packet is in there."

"Either way, I think it confirms that someone kept reptiles here," Harriet said. "Why, I don't know. It's awful. Not even a window for natural light."

Van put the scrap in an evidence bag. "This place was probably a temporary holding pen. It's out of the way, with no nosy neighbors and no way for anyone without a key to see inside."

"Think the nephew is involved?" Jason asked.

"It's possible," Van said. "Let's stop by Isaac Dinsdale's again. I'll show him what we found and have him sign off on it."

"He'll probably think you're nuts," Harriet said. "Asking about a scrap of trash."

Van wiggled the bag. "A very specific piece of trash. This could solve the whole case."

"What? How?" Jason asked. "You think whoever dropped that also hit me?" His hand went to his bandage.

"Seems likely to me." Van tucked the evidence bag in his larger investigating kit. "There's a bigger picture here. I think this place might have been used by smugglers. You happened to come along right when they were either visiting the reptiles or moving them out."

"They might have thought you were onto them, Jason," Harriet said. "Especially if they recognized you as an exotic animal vet."

Jason's face paled. "I guess I'm lucky it wasn't worse. They could have killed me."

When Van didn't reassure him immediately, a chill went down Harriet's spine. Desperate people did desperate things. Smugglers had a lot to lose if they were caught.

"I respect you both greatly," Van said. "I admire your dedication to caring for animals. I have to say this though. Be careful. We're going to find these people. When we do, they might lash out. I don't want either of you on their radar."

CHAPTER TWENTY-THREE

"Think we'll have any luck tonight?" Polly asked Harriet the next evening on their drive to Whitby for the local reptile enthusiast meeting.

"I sure hope so. I feel like we're inching toward the truth." Harriet was glad Polly was driving. It had been a long and busy day, with back-to-back appointments from open to close. Thinking of the talk she was giving, a last-minute request from Eddie, she checked her bag for her notes. There they were. *Phew.*

"The scrap from the packet was a find," Polly said. "And the rest of it was in the trash bag. It was so clever of Van to think of checking for it."

"A stroke of luck for sure. Now we know someone had reptiles inside the building. I wish they'd still been there so we could have rescued them."

"I know. That would have been great." They had reached the outskirts of Whitby, and Polly slowed. "According to the directions, our turn is coming up."

"The Angler's Inn...?" Harriet consulted her phone. "Yes. The next right."

Polly rounded the corner, and they saw the pub, a two-story building of white stone with black shutters. "We're in the annex, right?"

Harriet checked the directions Eddie had sent. "Yes. We go in around back, behind the main building." She pointed. "There's a parking spot. On the end."

Polly slid into the space. "Perfect. We can make a quick getaway."

"I hope we don't need to," Harriet said. Her pulse gave a leap. What if the smugglers were at this meeting? Not that they'd be identified as such. She pictured a name tag with *Smuggler* written on it and laughed.

"What's so funny?" Polly shut off the car and searched around for her handbag. Harriet explained, which drew a laugh from Polly as well. "Too bad it's not that easy to identify them."

The evening was getting chilly, and Harriet was glad she'd worn a fleece jacket. As they strolled through the parking lot, she saw a man carrying a small cage approach the entrance. There was something familiar about him, but she couldn't put her finger on it.

When he passed under the glow of the outside light, she recognized him. "That's Officer Crosby." He was dressed in jeans and a jacket, and it had taken her a bit to recognize him without his uniform.

"Really?" Polly asked. "What's he doing here?"

"He had a cage with him. Maybe he brought his pet." Though the officer had never indicated a personal interest in reptiles. Not that she'd spent much time talking to him. He was pretty much all business.

Harriet's steps faltered. What if he was here to track down the smugglers too?

"What is it?" Polly asked.

Harriet put a hand on Polly's arm. "Pretend you don't know him, okay? Unless he approaches us. He might be working undercover."

"Good call. We certainly don't want to blow it for him."

Inside the front door, they encountered a sign-in table. The room beyond was filled with chattering guests, standing in groups or seated at tables. Many had brought cages and were showing people their pets.

"Quite a crowd," Harriet said. She and Polly stood back until Officer Crosby and another person had signed in. Then they went forward.

"You made it." Eddie was seated behind the table, and he gave them a big smile.

"Of course," Harriet said. "You still want me to give a talk?"

"Please. It would be so appreciated." He pointed at the page. "You can sign in here."

As Harriet scrawled her name, she spotted *Darren Crosby* written on a line above. So, if he was here to investigate, he wasn't hiding his identity. Good to know. Next, she wrote her name on a sticker and pressed it on her chest.

Polly was signing the page when the outside door opened again, admitting Ruth Armstrong and Jason Peel.

"What are you two doing here?" Harriet asked, astonished. Jason hadn't said a word about attending this meeting when she'd brought it up. She glanced back and forth between them. "Did you come together?"

"No." Ruth laughed. "We ran into each other in the parking lot."

"So you've met." Harriet was still grappling with this unexpected pairing. Were they telling the truth? They seemed awfully chummy for a random encounter. She remembered the photo of Ruth at the reptile show in Germany. Had Jason been the man with her?

Harriet tried to ignore the doubts intruding on her thoughts. Questioning the actions of a new friend made her feel squeamish. Still, a glance at Polly informed her that she shared Harriet's questions.

"We met at the zoo," Jason said. "When Ruth was protesting."

The young woman rolled her eyes. "Those days are over." She glanced around the room. "For the most part. Still not happy when people keep wildlife as pets. Or buy smuggled animals, especially endangered ones."

"I agree with you there." Harriet wondered if Ruth would spot any guilty parties tonight. She hoped Ruth wouldn't make a scene and upset people. Eddie, for instance. He was a good example of a responsible pet owner, as far as she knew. "How are you feeling, Jason?"

"Better and better. The doctor cleared me to drive. I'm heading back to York tomorrow."

"That's good to hear," Harriet said. "The driving, I mean. It's been nice having you around."

"So, Harriet," Ruth said, "what are you doing here? You didn't bring a reptile."

"I'm here to give a talk," Harriet said. "Unless you'd like to step in, Jason? You're much more of an expert than I am."

"No, no. I'm sure you'll do fine. I'll take a few questions from the audience, though, if you'd like."

Harriet turned to Eddie, who had been listening in. "Eddie, this is Dr. Jason Peel. He's an exotic animal vet."

Eddie popped out of his chair and came around to shake Jason's hand. "It's so nice to meet you. Everyone will be thrilled you're here. I'm sure plenty of them would love to be able to pick your brain."

"Thanks for the warm welcome," Jason said. "You've got a good group tonight."

Eddie surveyed the room. "A lot of people came out. Everyone loves to show off their pets." He went over to the table and grabbed a cage from beneath it. "I brought Curtis, my chameleon."

"He's beautiful," Ruth said, going over to admire him.

His owner beamed with pride. "Isn't he?"

"Absolutely gorgeous." Ruth poked her finger through a gap in the wires.

"Oh, don't do that. He doesn't like being touched," Eddie said.

"Sorry." Ruth withdrew her hand.

"Yeah, be careful," Jason warned. "Some reptiles bite." He glanced around the room. "Please excuse me. I need to talk to someone."

Curious to see who, Harriet watched as he crossed the room, but he was soon lost in the crowd.

Ruth also slipped away, heading toward a group admiring a corn snake.

"How will this go, Eddie?" Polly asked.

Eddie glanced at a wall clock. "I'll call the meeting to order in a few minutes and then introduce Harriet. After her talk, it's back to mix-and-mingle. Refreshments will be served buffet style. Hot and cold drinks, cheese and crackers, crisps and dip, sweets."

Other attendees were coming through the door, so Harriet and Polly let Eddie return to his station. They wandered through the room, stopping to admire various pets. Everyone was friendly and happy to share.

"I had no idea there were so many reptile owners around," Harriet said.

"Well, it's not like they walk them," Polly said.

Harriet laughed. "True." That was part of the issue with smuggled reptiles. Unless people bragged or shared pictures online, who would know where they were?

Did someone here have Mango? She scanned the group, a mix of people from all walks of life, but everyone appeared normal to her.

Harriet wondered if Isaac Dinsdale's nephew, Craig, was there. Isaac claimed that his nephew had been using the crofter's hut. It made sense that Craig might know who had kept the reptiles there.

Too bad she hadn't been more attentive to the registration list.

But she might have a connection that would be even more useful. Eddie was still at the table, checking paperwork. "Polly, I'm going to talk to Eddie for a sec."

"Okay," Polly said. "I'll track down Jason."

Harriet hurried over to the reception table. She wanted to catch Eddie before he decided to open the meeting.

"Hey, Eddie." Harriet slid into the second chair at the table. "Any luck with what we talked about the other day?" Meaning getting information about the smugglers. Since then, there had been several developments, with Jason being attacked and the discovery that reptiles had been housed in the crofter's hut. Neither of which she intended to discuss with Eddie. She had to keep that information to herself so as not to jeopardize the investigation.

Eddie lowered his voice. "Nothing definite yet. Though I've been hearing some chatter about the reptile show next weekend in York. I think some shady characters might be attending."

"They sell at shows?"

"All the time. You have to know the right people—well, the wrong ones. Cash only."

"How do you find these people?" Harriet asked. She could make plans to go, along with Van and whoever else wanted to come.

Maybe they would find Mango.

Eddie glanced in both directions. "I'll put out some feelers, okay? Someone usually knows something." He drummed his fingers on the table. "The thing is, no one cared before. We'd report stuff, but no one followed up."

"That's frustrating," Harriet said. In fact, Officer Crosby himself must have been the source of frustration. Was he overworked? Or were such cases not considered a priority? Both could be true.

She thought of Craig Dinsdale. Someone keeping smuggled reptiles in the crofter's hut didn't mean he was directly involved. Maybe someone had paid him to turn a blind eye to what they were doing.

Should she ask Eddie about him? It was risky. What if they were good friends and Eddie tipped Craig off? No, she'd better let Van take the lead with Craig.

Eddie pushed back his chair. "It's time to start. You ready?"

Harriet let her questions go. She needed to focus on her talk.

Eddie went to a small podium set up at the other end of the room. "Hello, everyone," he called out. The room quieted. "I'm so glad to see you all here tonight. Even more so to see your reptiles." Laughter and cheers broke out. "Anyway, we have a special treat this evening. Dr. Harriet Bailey, who runs a veterinarian clinic in White Church Bay, is going to speak to us. Dr. Bailey, come on up."

Conscious of all the eyes on her, Harriet joined him at the podium.

"We also have another vet in the house tonight. Dr. Jason Peel specializes in exotic animal care and has generously offered to answer questions."

Everyone clapped. Jason, who was seated near the front, stood and waved. Harriet noticed that Polly sat to his right. When she caught her friend's eye, Polly subtly shifted her gaze toward the young man on her right. His name tag read *Craig Dinsdale*. On Craig's other side, Ruth leaned close to him and whispered something.

Tingles raced up Harriet's spine. Were Ruth and Craig connected? And what about Jason? Did he know Craig too?

Harriet nodded to Polly to acknowledge that she'd received the silent message, then began. "Hello, everyone. It's wonderful to be here. I'm really enjoying meeting you and your pets, as is Polly Thatcher, my wonderful assistant. Polly, stand up." Polly obeyed, waving at the crowd. Harriet gave a little background on the clinic and then began her talk.

The subject was signs of distress in reptiles. She covered behavior, changes in eating habits, and other indicators of injury or illness. At the end, she thanked everyone and invited Jason up to field questions. Harriet took his vacated seat.

The exotic animal vet was well-spoken and soon had the audience enthralled with a lively discussion.

"Good job," Polly whispered to her.

"Thanks," Harriet whispered back. As she turned her attention to Jason, she caught Craig staring at her. When she met his eye, he gave her a glare before turning away.

What was that all about? Had his uncle told him about their visit to the crofter's hut? She couldn't think of another reason why he would be so hostile.

Harriet didn't like to make snap judgments about people. However, in this case, she couldn't help feeling that Craig Dinsdale was not a nice person.

When the questions petered out, the general meet-and-greet resumed. Polly and Harriet meandered to the buffet for cups of tea and cookies.

"What do you think so far?" Polly asked as she dispensed hot water from a large carafe over tea bags in to-go cups.

"I'm seeing some interesting connections." Harriet leaned close. "I'll fill you in later."

Polly handed her a cup. "I didn't get a chance to see what Officer Crosby had in his cage."

The Border Force agent was seated at a table, the cage next to him.

"Let's go." Harriet carried the tea in one hand, a napkin with cookies in the other.

Officer Crosby shifted in his chair when he saw them approaching. "I didn't expect to see you here, Dr. Bailey."

"And I didn't expect to see you," Harriet said lightly. She peered into the cage, admiring the black-and-white lizard inside.

The officer softened. "His name is Spot. He's a leopard gecko."

"He's adorable," Polly said. "Is he easy to care for?"

"Very." Crosby gave them particulars about the species and why they were popular pets. He was so enthusiastic that Harriet almost wanted to get one for herself.

The encounter was pleasant, so Harriet had to steel herself to bring up a difficult topic. "Have you been able to follow up on Mango?" she asked.

The officer's jaw set in a stubborn line. "Dr. Peel already asked me that. No, I have not. Like I told you, the left hand doesn't know what the right hand is doing over there most of the time."

"All right," Harriet said. "If you get a chance, can you check? I want to make sure she gets home safely."

His response was an noncommittal grunt, and when other people approached, he turned to them with an eager greeting. Thus dismissed, Harriet and Polly wandered away.

"It's probably time to get going," Harriet said as she tossed her empty cup and napkin in the trash.

Polly suppressed a yawn. "Sure. I'm going to visit the loo first."

"Me too." Harriet followed Polly through a door into a hallway where the restrooms were located. There was a line.

While they waited, Harriet reflected on the events of the evening. They definitely needed to attend the reptile show. And find out how Craig Dinsdale knew Ruth—who was currently exiting the restroom.

On impulse, Harriet left the line. "Ruth, can I talk to you for a second?"

Ruth smiled at her. "Sure."

"Through here." Harriet went back into the main room, where they were less likely to be overheard.

"What's up?" Ruth asked.

"You're working for Nick now, right?" Harriet asked. Victoria hadn't heard from her brother for days, and if Harriet could give her some reassurance, she would. "How's it going?"

Ruth shrugged. "Fine. I'm in the office. I take care of orders, paying bills, depositing checks, updating the website, whatever they need."

"It must be interesting. From what I've seen, they sell nice things."

Her eyes lit up. "They sure do. Nick's been traveling around Yorkshire lining up new retail outlets. The business is growing like crazy."

Maybe that was why Victoria hadn't heard from him. He was busy building his business. Harriet would pass that information along. Now for the difficult part. "How do you know Craig Dinsdale?"

Ruth's brows drew together. "We work together."

"He works for Voyager Imports?" Harriet hadn't expected that answer.

"In the warehouse. He also makes deliveries to stores." Ruth folded her arms. "Why?"

Harriet almost dropped the subject at the suspicion in her tone. Then she recalled Craig's ugly glare for someone he'd never met before, as well as the knowledge that reptiles had been kept in an isolated hut he had access to.

"Be careful," Harriet told Ruth. "That's all I'm going to say. Okay?"

Then she walked away before she thought better of it.

CHAPTER TWENTY-FOUR

I can't believe it's Friday." Polly pushed back from her desk. "What a busy week it's been."

Harriet studied the schedule. "We have a couple of appointments after lunch. Then we're off the rest of the day. Unless we get a—"

The phone rang. Harriet and Polly laughed. "What were you about to say?" Polly asked with a cheeky grin as she grabbed the receiver.

Harriet leafed through the upcoming files, half-listening to Polly. Tomorrow the clinic would be closed so they could attend the York reptile show. She'd passed along the information she'd gleaned at the reptile owner's gathering to Van, and he'd promised to keep them posted with any developments.

She hadn't heard from him. Reason told her there must not be any news yet, but anxiety twisted her stomach. Would they ever find the smugglers? What about Mango? Jason had checked with the Wildlife Crimes Unit again, and they still didn't know where the iguana was. She hadn't bothered to call Officer Crosby.

"You can come in now," Polly was saying. "Yes. She has time."

Harriet held back a groan. Maybe she could eat a sandwich before the patient arrived. She was starving.

Polly hung up. "You'll never believe who this patient is."

"I can't guess." Then Harriet's heart gave a jolt. "Is it Mango?"

"No, but close. Cassandra Willis is bringing in a female genet."

Horrible understanding dawned. "The one missing from the zoo?"

"I don't know, but I think we should ask her where she got it," Polly said. "They're not exactly sold in pet stores."

"I will." Harriet glanced at the clock. "I'm going to run and grab a sandwich. Want something?"

"No thanks. I packed my lunch today."

Harriet carried her lunch back to the clinic, and they ate together. "Remember when we saw Cassandra eating with Nick and Ozzie?" Harriet asked.

"I do. It makes sense that one of them might have stolen the genet. Not many people have access."

Harriet pulled out her phone. "I'm tempted to call Victoria."

"Not yet," Polly cautioned. "Cassandra might have bought it somewhere else. We don't know that it's the same animal."

"I suppose." Harriet finished her sandwich. "I'd better go wash up."

By the time she returned, Cassandra Willis was in the waiting room. She jumped up when she saw Harriet. "Thanks so much for taking me. I wasn't sure if you'd see Penelope." She picked up the cage, ready to follow Harriet to the exam room.

"Penelope, huh?" Harriet eyed the mammal with its spotted coat and pointed nose. "She's beautiful."

"Isn't she? I guess I have a theme going with my pets. I adore spotted animals."

"How long have you had her?" Harriet asked, in what she hoped was a casual manner.

"A few days."

Harriet's pulse leaped. The timeframe worked. Once they were inside the exam room, she had Cassandra set the cage on the table. "What seems to be the problem?" Harriet opened the cage door, but the genet didn't react. She merely sat and blinked at her.

"She's not acting right," Cassandra said. "I know it's daytime and they're nocturnal, but she hasn't been moving around at all. She's also not eating much, even though I've been careful to give her the right food."

Harriet put on thick gloves and gently eased the creature out of the cage. Surprisingly, Penelope didn't resist, and Harriet was able to examine her. She didn't find any signs of illness or injury besides the lethargy.

"I'm going to call someone," she said. "I need some advice."

Cassandra frowned. "You don't know what's wrong?"

"Not off the top of my head. Her eyes are clear, her mouth looks okay. She doesn't seem to be in any pain, and while I'm grateful for that, it doesn't give me any direction about what might be going on with her. My expertise is more with domestic animals, so I want to seek advice from a colleague rather than guess."

"I appreciate that."

Harriet started for the door then hesitated. She ought to ask her question now, while she was on decent terms with Cassandra. "Where did you get her?"

"What do you mean?"

"If it was a dealer, we could call them. They'll have a history on Penelope."

Cassandra wrung her hands. "She was a gift from a friend. A rescue, actually. Do you think she was mistreated at her previous home?"

"I certainly hope not." Even though Harriet grew more concerned with every answer Cassandra gave her, she felt it wouldn't be appropriate or professional to ask for the friend's name. "I'll be back shortly. Please make yourself comfortable."

Harriet ducked out of the exam room and placed the call in her office, with the door shut. "Jason," she said, "I'm so glad you answered. I've got somewhat of a situation here."

"That sounds intriguing. What's going on?"

She swiftly filled him in. "I'm stumped. The genet seems healthy."

"Genets don't bond easily with humans," Jason explained. "Which means they don't do well when they're rehomed. They can get depressed when they're taken away from their original owner."

"That might be it. Cassandra said she was a rescue."

"That doesn't mean the animal was mistreated. A lot of times the previous owner doesn't want the animal anymore. That happens frequently with exotic pets. People get tired of the specialty care when the novelty wears off."

"I've seen that with non-exotic animals as well, unfortunately," Harriet said. "Where do we go from here?"

Jason was quiet for a moment. "If returning her isn't an option, then a lot of patience is required for the genet to get comfortable with her new owner. I can work with Cassandra if she wants."

"I'll suggest it," Harriet said, relieved. "How do you think the genet would do with other genets? I mean, assuming she doesn't adapt to her new home."

"Being with other genets would be more natural and therefore easier for her to adapt to. I think that's a good backup plan."

"All right. I'll pass your offer along. Thanks so much for your input." Before ending the call, she asked, "By the way, are you still planning to attend the reptile show? We're going."

"I am. Let's connect by text in the morning."

Harriet wanted to tell him what Eddie had said but decided not to say too much. She was almost positive she could trust Jason. Almost. "I'll let you get back to work. Thanks again."

"No problem. Call anytime." With that cheerful sign-off, Jason was gone.

Cassandra rose to her feet when Harriet entered. "What did your colleague say?"

There wasn't any way to beat around the bush. "He told me it's not healthy for genets to be rehomed. Being away from the owner and environment they're used to can make them depressed. Since we don't have any indicators that there's something physically wrong with her, I'm inclined to believe that's the case with Penelope."

"Depressed?" Cassandra's gaze flew to her pet. "That's awful. What can we do?"

"Well, the best thing would be to return her to the original owner," Harriet said gently. "Can you contact whoever gave you the genet and explain?"

Cassandra laced her fingers together. "I can try. What if my friend refuses to take her back?"

"Then Dr. Jason Peel, an exotic animal vet, will work with you and the genet to monitor the situation. We also have another option if things get dire." Harriet jotted down Jason's contact info on a notepad and handed the page to Cassandra. "Here's his number."

"Thank you." Cassandra tucked the note inside her bag and then stood. "Is there anything else?"

"Keep me posted, please," Harriet suggested. "The referral doesn't mean I don't care. I'm very interested in Penelope's welfare."

"Okay. I'll do that." Cassandra picked up the cage and hurried through the exam room door.

Harriet took a moment to breathe. She'd been so sure Cassandra's genet had come from the zoo. The mention of a rescue had thrown her off. All of Moorland Zoo's animals were well cared for and didn't need to be rescued.

On the other hand, an animal activist might think otherwise.

"Harriet?" Polly stood in the doorway. "Your next appointment is waiting."

"Sorry." Harriet did her best to shrug off her troubled thoughts. "I'm on my way. I'll fill you in later."

"Later" ended up being after-hours, sitting with tea at the back table in the garden. Victoria was there, at Harriet's request, and she'd said she also had an update to share.

"So, who's first?" Polly's ponytail swung as she glanced between her companions.

Victoria gestured to Harriet. "Go ahead, please."

Harriet took a breath. "A client came in today with a genet."

Victoria sat up straight, her eyes wide. "What? My genet?"

"I don't know for sure," Harriet said. "Let me tell you what happened."

While Polly and Victoria listened in fascination, Harriet relayed every twist and turn of Cassandra's visit to the clinic. Although Polly knew the client's name, Harriet didn't mention it to Victoria. It wouldn't be appropriate at this point, especially if Cassandra was innocent.

Once Harriet was finished, Victoria hummed in thought for a moment. "The genet was healthy and female, like mine. But your client claimed she was a rescue?"

"Yes, and that threw me off at first. Then I got to thinking. We know one person who thinks zoos are inhumane and who might think of an animal that had been 'liberated' from a zoo as a rescue."

Victoria's lips pressed into a firm line. "Ruth. Does she know your client?"

Harriet thought about seeing Cassandra out with Ruth, Nick, and Ozzie. "It's possible," she said. On the other hand, Nick, Ozzie, and Cassandra were also suspects. "That's all I can say. I'll fill Van in and see what he wants to do. Let him question the client. I wanted to ask more questions, believe me. But it wouldn't have been appropriate. It could be an entirely different animal. I didn't want to accuse her of something she didn't do or spook her if she was guilty."

"I understand," Victoria said. "I'll wait for Van to handle it. As long as the client is taking care of her."

"She'll be consulting Dr. Peel, so I'd say yes."

"I agree." Victoria thought for a moment. "Well, that was quite a bombshell. Now it's time for mine. Actually, it's more of a recovered memory that shocked me." Her lips twisted. "Oddly, it also involves Ruth."

"What is it?" Polly asked eagerly.

"This morning, when I woke up, a memory came to me, as clearly as if it happened yesterday." Victoria shook her head. "It wasn't a dream. I remembered how many pictures I used to draw showing Nick coming home and giving me a big hug. How strongly I believed it would happen." She opened her handbag and pulled out a drawing created by a childish hand. "My dad kept this one in his desk. I think it, and hearing Ruth talk about the giraffe, brought it all back."

The drawing depicted two figures outside a house, one male, the other female. They were hugging, and little Victoria had drawn hearts all over the page.

Victoria's gaze grew distant. "It was a day or two after the sailboat sank. I was in Dad's study, hiding behind a chair. I liked to sit in there to be close to my dad. Ruth came in to talk to Dad. She said something about the giraffe. I remember, because I always liked it too."

Harriet realized she was literally sitting on the edge of her seat.

"Ruth told Dad she'd seen Nick on the docks. Not before the storm, like we always thought, but *during* it."

Harriet gasped. "She told me the storm was just brewing when Nick set off. But if he was on the docks in the middle of the storm, that means he wasn't on the sailboat when it sank."

"Talk about dropping a bomb," Harriet mused to Polly while beating eggs for breakfast the next morning. "I was thinking about it all night."

Will was due any minute, and after the meal, they were headed to the reptile show in York. Van would meet them there, having decided to take his official vehicle. He was optimistic that there would be arrests and was coordinating with the local force. After the show, he intended to investigate the genet.

"Me too." Polly slid slices of bread into the toaster. "No wonder her dad waited so long to have him declared dead. He believed Ruth and was hopeful that Nick would return."

"But why didn't he, either after the boat sank or at any point during the next twenty years?" Harriet was both puzzled and frustrated on Victoria's behalf. The story could have had a completely different ending.

Polly started the toaster. "Something must have happened on the boat. I think Nick blames himself for what happened to his cousin."

Someone rapped on the back door, rousing a yip from Maxwell, who scrambled to see who it was.

"That must be Will." Harriet poured the eggs into a hot pan. "Can you let him in?"

Polly hurried to answer, and a moment later, Will followed her into the room.

"Good morning," he said cheerfully, coming over to give Harriet a kiss on the cheek. He peered into the pan. "Those look good."

Harriet smiled. "I hope you're hungry. We also have bacon, and Polly is making toast."

The toast popped, and Polly grabbed the slices then smoothed butter over the surfaces. "Hope you like butter on your toast, Will."

"I'm not fussy when someone is cooking for me," he said.

They soon sat down to the meal, Will offering grace before they dug in.

"We have marmalade or strawberry jam for your toast," Harriet said, passing him the jam holder. "We also had an interesting conversation with Victoria yesterday. Oh, and we now have a genet as a patient. Remember how one is missing from the zoo?"

Will raised an eyebrow as he layered jam on his toast. "Can't leave you alone for a minute, can I?"

"I don't think we reported to you about the reptile meeting either," Harriet said.

Will had been busy all week, and they'd only communicated via text and a short conversation after Bible study on Wednesday evening. Other parishioners had been hanging around, so she hadn't been able to say much then.

"Take it from the top," Will said. "I want every detail."

Between Harriet and Polly, they managed to eat while giving him the updates. As with Victoria, Harriet didn't mention Cassandra's name.

Will got the gist and was excited that they might retrieve the zoo's missing animal. "If Ruth actually did see Nick on the dock during the storm," he said, "that puts a whole new spin on things."

"Marshall eventually went ahead and filed the declaration of death," Harriet pointed out. "Probably after an extensive search. Being so young, Victoria wasn't privy to those efforts, I'm guessing."

"The poor man." Will scooped up a bite of eggs. "Why didn't Nick come back? He must have known how painful the ordeal was for his family."

"Polly and I have been wondering that too," Harriet said. "Maybe he'll get up the gumption to tell his sister what actually happened that night. As it stands now, he'll have to appeal to the court for his share. They may not award it to him."

The clinic phone rang. Harriet put down her fork with a groan. She really wanted to attend the reptile show.

"You could let it go to voice mail," Will suggested.

"No, I can't. It could be an emergency." Harriet got up and went to answer. "Dr. Bailey here."

"Harriet?" a woman inquired. She sounded as if she was crying.

"Yes. Who is this?" Harriet could barely hear her.

"Ruth. Ruth Armstrong. I need your help. Please. The smugglers. I'm at the Voyager Imports warehouse. It's at—"

"I know where it is," Harriet interrupted. "We'll be right there."

CHAPTER TWENTY-FIVE

Harriet hung up and grabbed her dishes from the table. "We need to go. It's about the smuggling, and it's urgent."

The trio hopped into the Land Rover and set off toward the village. "You know where we're going?" Will asked.

"I do. I checked the place out the other day." Harriet snorted. "Being nosy paid off."

"Doesn't it always?" Polly quipped. "Did she say what's going on?"

"No," Harriet said. "She was crying, so I could barely understand her."

"Something to do with the reptile smuggling though." Will rubbed his chin. "Do you think Ozzie and perhaps Nick are involved?"

"Maybe. It makes sense," Harriet reluctantly admitted. "An import business? Plus, they used to export when they lived in South Africa." The thought was sickening. "Victoria is going to be heartbroken if it's true."

Not only was smuggling a crime, it decimated local populations and put vulnerable reptiles at risk physically. Many didn't survive, especially since the way they were transported was covert and often inadequate to their needs.

Harriet drove as fast as she dared along the narrow, winding road to town. "Polly, want to call Van?"

"Will do." Polly made the call, and Harriet was relieved to hear her having an actual conversation rather than leaving a message.

The parking lot at the warehouse was empty. Harriet pulled in and lurched to an abrupt stop. They jumped out of the vehicle and hurried toward the building entrance.

"I wonder where Ruth is." Harriet tested the front door and found it open.

They were in a small office, which had a desk and a few chairs for visitors. A bigger office was visible through an open door. To one side was another door that Harriet guessed led to the rest of the building.

Harriet went to that door, which was also unlocked. "Ruth? Ruth, where are you?" she called as she stepped into a corridor. Now she was getting worried. What if Ruth had been attacked, the way Jason had been?

"She must be in the warehouse," Will said, gesturing toward the plate glass window on the left wall. Through the window, pallets and shelves of goods stood in a vast, shadowy room.

Harriet hurried through yet another door into the warehouse. "Ruth," she shouted.

From the distance, a faint voice replied, "I'm back here. Go straight, and you'll find me."

She found Ruth standing in a room furnished only with shelving. A trash can overflowed with items that were all too familiar—packaged food wrappers and old bedding materials.

"What's going on?" Harriet asked, even though she was afraid she knew.

"This room." Ruth gestured. "They were keeping reptiles here. I saw Craig Dinsdale loading them into a company van."

A shout came from the warehouse. "That must be Van. Polly, will you go get him? He'll want to hear this."

Van and Polly soon returned, the DC all business. "Okay, Miss Armstrong. Start at the beginning."

Ruth explained how the room had always been kept locked. She hadn't thought much of it until Officer Crosby had visited several times, disappearing into the room with Craig and Ozzie for an hour or more at a time.

"Not Nick?" Harriet interrupted.

"No. He's been away." Ruth showed them a set of keys. "I finally decided I was going to get inside this room and find out what was going on. I came over early this morning when no one was supposed to be here. I saw Craig, with the van parked near the back. No merchandise was supposed to go out, so I spied on him. I thought maybe he was stealing from the company." Tears sparkled in her eyes. "Instead, he was carrying out crates of snakes and lizards and iguanas. They didn't look very good. They were all droopy, lying on the bottom of their cages."

Harriet felt heartsick. "Where is he taking them? Do you know?"

Van set his jaw. "The reptile show, no doubt." He turned to Ruth. "Can you get me the registration number for the van? We'll put out a bulletin for it."

Ruth perked up. "I can get it for you. It's in the office."

"Thanks," Van said. "And lock this room. I don't want anyone in here until I have a chance to go through it."

They went out to the parking lot. "I'll meet you at the show," Van said. "Miss Armstrong, can you go to the show with Harriet? I need you to point Craig out to us."

Harriet was relieved by this suggestion. She had seen Craig only once, at the reptile gathering.

Ruth nodded. "I'll do anything to help."

Soon they were on their way to the reptile show in York. Van led the way in the cruiser, and Harriet stayed on his tail, confident that she wouldn't get stopped.

"I have something to tell you," Ruth said with a sniffle. She was in the passenger seat, with Will and Polly sitting in back. "I did something bad."

Harriet's heart skipped a beat. "What is it, Ruth? We're all your friends here."

Ruth nibbled at her lower lip. "You know that iguana you found? I let her go a couple of weeks ago. That's why she was roaming around loose." Her hands twisted together in her lap. "I know now I never should have done that." She gulped. "I let the snake go too. The same night."

Harriet glanced in the rearview mirror at her friends, who looked equally shocked. "Where did you let them go from?"

"Officer Crosby's car." Ruth sighed. "It was totally on impulse. One night I was out for a walk, and I went by his house." She explained where the officer lived, in the upper village near the coast path. "He was moving cages from his Border Force van to his personal car, which I thought was strange. Where was he taking them? It seemed underhanded to me."

Harriet agreed. If Officer Crosby had intercepted smugglers in the course of his official duties, the animals should have been handled by the book. Like when he'd taken Mango away to await return to her home overseas. Or so he claimed.

The Wildlife Crimes Unit said they didn't have her. After what Ruth had said, Harriet had a strong feeling that Officer Crosby had never turned her in.

Ruth went on. "I stood by the hedge and watched him. Then he got a phone call. He walked away, talking, and I ran over to find out what he was doing."

Polly sucked in a breath. "That was risky."

"When you're an activist, you learn to take risks," Ruth said. "Anyway, he had reptiles in the cages. So I opened two and let them out. I could hardly get away with the cages, and I figured if they'd come from the wild, they'd be able to take care of themselves better than I could. Maybe Officer Crosby would think he'd simply forgotten to latch the cages. I didn't think about how they were probably in a totally different environment than they were used to. They took off, and then I did too, right before he came back." She paused and then added, "That's one reason I got suspicious when he started hanging around the warehouse."

Harriet forced down the scolding words that rose to her lips. Ruth appeared to have learned her lesson, and a lecture would only create a wedge between them.

Instead, she said, "I'm glad you made the connection with Officer Crosby. Otherwise, they might have gotten away with it." She'd never warmed to the Border Force agent. He'd been brusque and unfriendly, probably to keep her at arm's length. She thought of his leopard gecko. As a pet owner himself, she would have thought he'd see the harm smuggling caused.

"Did you see any other iguanas like Mango?" Harriet asked.

"The one you let go?"

"There might have been another one or two like that," Ruth said. "It was pretty dark, so I can't say for sure."

A high-value shipment for sure then. Harriet hoped Mango's fellow iguanas were still healthy. Maybe they'd find all of them at the show. Officer Crosby might have already sold Mango though. Her heart sank at the thought.

The reptile show was being held at an event center surrounded by acres of parking lot. Signs directed them to the entrance for the reptile exhibit. Harriet parked beside Van's cruiser. He got out and came over to the window. "I'm going to circle the building to see if I can spot the Voyager Imports van. Can you describe it, Ruth?"

"It's white, with the logo painted on both sides." Ruth fumbled in her handbag. "The logo is on the business card." She handed it to Harriet, who passed it to Van.

Van studied the card. "Okay, you ready? I want us to stick together." He went back to his car and set off.

Harriet followed as they drove slowly through the parking lot and around the building. They had reached the rear, where there were loading docks, when Ruth spotted the van. "There it is. Right by that door. See?"

Van pulled up close to the door and got out to try to open it. Shaking his head, he trotted over to them. "It's locked. Listen, I'm going to talk to the security staff here and get a map. There must be another way into that area."

They traveled around to the front and once again drove up near the show entrance. This time they all got out. As the group walked across the lot, Van made a call on his phone. "I'm going to have officers from the local department join me. I'm on their turf, and I could use the help. I have no idea what we're walking into here."

"What can we do?" Harriet asked.

Van considered. "Once we're inside, see if you can spot Nick Langford, Craig Dinsdale, Ozzie Bright, or Officer Crosby. Don't let on what we're doing here, but keep an eye on them, okay? Send me a text if you find them. And I'll keep in touch the same way." Van turned to Harriet. "While you're at it, keep an eye out for any exotic species that might have been smuggled in. Birds of a feather might be flocking together here, right?"

"I'll do my best." Harriet wasn't especially well-versed in which reptile species were smuggled rather than native, but she would try. "We have a contact here who might help."

"Yes, Eddie Agar," Polly said. "He'll be here, along with a lot of people from the local group. I know a few faces."

After they entered the venue, Van went over to the security guard and showed him his identification. The others continued to the sign-in table to buy tickets.

The exhibition hall was through two sets of double doors, a cavernous space echoing with voices. Booths had been set up in a grid, and along the wall, tables and chairs provided seating for visitors.

"Where to first?" Will asked, craning his neck.

"Let's start at one side and work our way around," Harriet suggested.

This was agreeable to everyone, so they started strolling past the booths, pausing occasionally to look more closely at the exhibits. There were a lot of reptiles for sale plus everything a pet owner might need: food, enclosures, toys, medications, treats, and cage accessories and supplies.

"The mission is underway," Polly said, reading from her phone. "They're going in the back room." She pointed. "It's in that corner."

"Let's go," Ruth said.

"Hold up," Harriet said, catching her sleeve. "We can't barge in there."

"I know," Ruth said. "But I'm not missing the action."

"Don't run," Polly said. "You'll attract too much attention."

They set off at a brisk yet unremarkable pace around the outer perimeter of the fair.

Harriet spotted Eddie, who was seated at a booth for his local group. He waved, and she noticed that he had his snake, Prunella, draped around his shoulders, not an uncommon sight at this event. Thinking he might have information, she stopped to talk, gesturing to the others that she'd catch up with them.

"How's it going?" she asked.

"Great. We're getting a lot of people signing up for our group's next meeting." Eddie tapped the page in front of him.

"Wonderful." Harriet glanced both ways then leaned over the table. "Any leads?"

His eyes lit with excitement. "A couple. There's supposed to be a VIP meeting with some rare reptiles. My friend is going to try to get me in."

"Good job." Harriet wondered if she should warn him off, in case it was the one that Van was about to raid. Well, if it was, she would vouch for him as an ally. "We're on the trail of something too. Hopefully we'll see you later."

Up ahead, the others rounded a corner and disappeared. As Harriet followed, she ran right into Ozzie Bright, Nick's business partner—and alleged reptile smuggler.

"Hello, Dr. Bailey," he said with a cheerful grin. "Fancy meeting you here." He loomed close, causing her to automatically step back.

Harriet forced herself to return his smile. She had to act as if nothing was wrong to avoid spooking him and ruining the raid. "I've gotten really interested in reptiles ever since rescuing the Bahamian iguana." She thought she saw him flinch at the mention of Mango. "They're fascinating creatures, aren't they?"

"If you say so." He frowned. "Was that Ruth I saw with Polly just now? What is she doing here?"

Leading the police to your operation. Harriet deliberately gave him a literal answer. "The same as us—checking out the exhibits."

A couple aisles away, Van and several officers in uniform headed toward the rear.

She shifted slightly so Ozzie's back would be to them. "Have you been to one of these shows before? I haven't, though I heard there was a good one in Germany recently."

"What do you know about Germany?" Ozzie's pleasant features twisted with anger, his blue eyes flashing.

"N-nothing," Harriet stuttered. She had been making conversation, saying whatever came into her mind. Then the photo she'd seen of Ruth in Germany flashed into her thoughts. Had she been talking to Ozzie? "Were you there?" she blurted.

Ozzie grabbed her forearm in a vice-like grip. "You've done enough meddling for one day, Dr. Bailey—"

Suddenly, he released her with a scream as a snake slid around his neck.

"Relax, mate," Eddie said from behind Ozzie. "Prunella doesn't bite. Unless you move in a way she doesn't like."

Snake in the Grass

"I don't like snakes," Ozzie gritted out, his eyes wide with fright. "Get her off me."

Knowing the worst he would get from a ball python's bite was an infection, Harriet fought a smile.

Eddie glanced at Harriet. "You need to be somewhere? I'll watch this one for you until security comes."

"Security?" Ozzie bellowed. "I didn't do anything."

"You grabbed my friend's arm in a distinctly unfriendly way," Eddie said. "That's assault."

Harriet backed up a couple steps. "Thanks, Eddie."

He flapped a hand at her. "Get a move on."

Around a corner or two, she caught up with her friends. "What happened to you?" Will asked. "I was about to come after you."

"I ran into Ozzie," Harriet said. "It wasn't exactly a pleasant encounter. I was trying to stop him from seeing Van. But Eddie and Prunella saved the day."

"The police went through to the back," Will said. "We thought it better to wait for permission to go in."

They paced close to the rear door, pretending to be interested in nearby exhibits.

Finally, the door opened, and Van beamed at them. "You want to come in? I have some good news."

"Oh, well done," Polly cried.

Van led the way, his shoes squeaking on the polished tile. "We got them. Craig Dinsdale, Darren Crosby, and a few buyers. Only one missing is the brains behind the operation, Ozzie Bright."

Harriet exchanged glances with her friends. "Um, he's tied up right now. With a snake."

"What?" Van stopped short, puzzled.

"My friend Eddie sicced his boa on him after Ozzie grabbed my arm. I bet security has him right now. Eddie was going to call."

"Good to know." Van dialed as he started walking again. "Walt? It's Van. That man charged with assault? Ozzie Bright? Yeah, don't let him go. Be there in a few."

Van led them to a room at the back of the building. A standing sign outside read, PRIVATE MEETING.

"They booked it as a sales meeting for the import company," Van explained. "The plan was to be in and out before security or anyone else got wind of what they were doing."

Beyond the room, the back door was open with police cruisers outside. Officers were assisting several men into the vehicles, including Craig and Officer Crosby.

The meeting room held about a dozen cages of various sizes, holding mostly iguanas and lizards, with a few snakes. "Judging by the price tags, some of these are very rare," Van said. "I've contacted Jason Peel, and he's going to help us take care of them."

Harriet's gaze was immediately drawn to a familiar iguana in a cage with several others. She'd recognize that lizard anywhere. Flooded with relief, Harriet hurried to the cage. A quick glance informed her that the iguana was in good condition. "Mango, you're okay! The twins will be so glad."

The iguana blinked at her, as if to ask, "What took you so long?"

CHAPTER TWENTY-SIX

A week later, Harriet was sitting in Victoria's kitchen, drinking coffee and chatting with her and Nick. In half an hour, Harriet and Victoria would drive to Manchester Airport to say goodbye to Mango and the other lizards before they flew home. The twins and their parents would meet them there.

"Nick's going to supervise the staff while we're gone," Victoria said. She patted her brother's hand. "You're getting quite fond of the zoo, aren't you?"

Her brother made a face. "I wouldn't go that far. I'd call it making the best of a bad situation." Then he gave his sister a smile that transformed his face. "I'm adjusting. Besides, I have Ruth for backup."

"Don't overwork the poor girl," Victoria said. "I need her."

Victoria had hired Ruth as the assistant zookeeper, a role she would grow into over the next year or so. She was taking college classes remotely and getting all kinds of hands-on experience. Her encounter with the reptile smugglers had transformed her views, and now she was channeling her passion for animals into advocacy and education through the zoo.

"Vic has always seen the best in everyone," Nick said. "Including me." His expression was rueful. "I can't believe you've actually forgiven me."

"I will always forgive you as long as you're honest with me," Victoria told him. "That's what family is for."

Nick had finally opened up to his sister and explained why he had stayed away so long.

The night of the sailboat sinking, he'd fought with his cousin about the stolen netsuke. Scott had dumped him on the dock and taken off, right into the teeth of the storm. Nick had been helpless to stop or save him. Blaming himself and fearing that his family would blame him too, he had stayed away from the house. After the storm, he'd hitched a ride to France on a fishing boat, and from there, he'd worked on freighters, then charter boats, finally landing in South Africa. A few years ago, he'd started a business—a legitimate export business—and when it became successful, he had decided to come home, hoping his father would forgive him if he could replace the pieces Scott had taken that night so many years before. But to his great sorrow, his father had died, never knowing that his son was alive.

Fortunately, he'd been able to provide enough information to prove to the police that Scott's injury was incurred during the shipwreck. However, his cousin's loss still haunted him, along with the fact that he'd never had a chance to reconcile with his father.

Ozzie, sensing money, had convinced him to claim his inheritance anyway. Ozzie had stolen the golden giraffe to help the new import business get off the ground. Fortunately, he hadn't had a chance to fence it yet, so Nick had been able to find it and return it to the family collection.

Ozzie had also taken the genet to impress Cassandra. His claim that it was a rescue had been an attempt to tug at her heartstrings. Cassandra had willingly returned the genet, and Harriet had gotten the impression that the zoo had a zealous new ally in her. Harriet was glad that Ruth hadn't stolen it from the zoo. Her new start there wouldn't be possible if she had.

As they'd suspected, Craig Dinsdale had supplied the crofter's shed to house the reptiles until they could be trafficked. He was also the one who attacked Jason that day on the trail.

"How's the business doing?" Harriet asked. "I bought some great dishes from you, by the way." She was going to use the colorful set, painted in a palm tree design, for summer meals.

"We're growing so fast," Nick said. "Now that I've got the books straightened out."

He'd discovered that Ozzie had been using the business account as his own personal checkbook. Fortunately, none of the smuggling proceeds had been funneled into the business. In a show of decency, Ozzie had cleared his former partner of all ties with the smuggling, so Nick had no lingering issues from Ozzie's arrest.

Darren Crosby was also facing charges, as more evidence was uncovered about smuggling activities going back years. His role was to receive the smuggled animals when they came in then disperse them to crooked dealers like the ones operating at the show.

"That's wonderful to hear," Harriet said. "We should get going, Victoria."

Victoria was smiling at her phone, her cheeks pink. "Sorry," she said, popping her phone into her handbag. "That was Jason. He's meeting us at the airport. He's going to give me a ride home."

"Sounds good." Harriet was glad things were going well for the pair. "Why don't we all have dinner one night soon?"

"I'd like that." Victoria slid off the stool. "Ready to go?"

"I am." Harriet carried her cup to the sink. "See you later, Nick."

"Bye, Harriet. Take good care of my kid sister, will you?"

"I am *not* a kid," Victoria protested.

Nick laughed and gave her a bear hug. "Maybe not, but you'll always be my kid sister."

As they headed out to the Land Rover, Victoria said, "We have a couple of extra minutes. Can I show you something?"

"Sure."

The golf cart was nearby, so they jumped on, and Victoria drove them to the snake house. "Remember how you were wondering if Slippery was a boy or girl?" she asked as they entered the building.

"Yes. Did you find out?"

"I'll say." Victoria's answer was to point to Slippery's cage, which now had a number of baby snakes slithering around.

"What a great surprise," Harriet said. "Slippery is a she."

"Jason has already helped me find homes for most of them," Victoria said.

"I'm sure Eddie would be happy to help with homes for the rest," Harriet said.

They drove the cart back to the parking lot then got on the road.

Manchester Airport was over two hours away. Harriet and Victoria passed the time talking, getting to know each other better and deepening their friendship.

Harriet had the feeling that she and Will would be spending quite a bit of time with Victoria and Jason on outings in the future. She was also glad to have another friend who was so passionate about animals.

"Okay, call me nosy, but what's up with Polly and Van?" Victoria asked. "I thought I sensed something there. Is it my imagination?"

"Not at all," Harriet said. "They are very good friends. It's complicated, but I hope they'll work it out." She thought they were on track to a reconciliation. That would be a happy day.

"They would make a fantastic couple," Victoria said. "I really like them both."

"Me too. We have a lot of fun together." Harriet recalled her feelings from a couple of weeks ago—full of spring fever, ready for new experiences and challenges.

That prayer had certainly been answered with abundance.

Signs appeared for the airport, and with Victoria's help, Harriet navigated to the cargo flights area. As they maneuvered into a parking space, Anthony and his family arrived. They pulled in right next to Harriet.

"Great timing," Harriet said, greeting them with hugs.

The twins immediately began chattering away to Victoria, asking her all kinds of questions about the animals at the zoo.

They easily found the designated hangar. "You must be the veterinarian and the zookeeper who helped us get these beauties back so we can send them home," said a Wildlife Crimes official by way of greeting.

"They're iguanas," Sebastian told her. "Very special ones."

"They are indeed," the woman said with a smile. "We're going to take very good care of them, I promise. They'll be loaded in a plane that will be taking off shortly. Do you want to watch?"

"Yes," the twins chorused.

The cargo official gave the adults directions on where to watch from. "It's time for them to go. Say goodbye."

Sebastian and Sophie knelt on the floor beside the cage. "You be a good girl, Mango," Sophie said. "And say hi to all your friends for us." Anthony took pictures while Olivia watched.

Harriet found that she was genuinely sad that Mango was leaving. She had actually gotten attached to a reptile.

Anthony finally peeled the twins away. The iguanas were wheeled across the tarmac to the plane, which was parked with its cargo doors open.

A short while later, as they stood at the fence, the aircraft taxied along, engines powering up.

"There she goes," Sebastian cried. He and Sophie waved as the plane lifted off, circled around, and was gone.

"Goodbye, Mango," Harriet whispered. "We'll never forget you."

FROM THE AUTHOR

Dear Reader,

I'm so glad to be back at Cobble Hill with you! In this adventure, Harriet steps outside of her comfort zone a bit. Not only does she find herself handling reptiles, but she also encounters exotic animals at a privately owned zoo. One patient requires Harriet to brush up on some rarely used skills.

While researching for this book, I came across fascinating information about zoos. While I was familiar with large, municipal zoos or small farm-based attractions such as petting zoos, I had no idea that there were so many that were privately owned. The first zoo in England was founded nine hundred years ago by Henry I, who built a wall to secure the lions, tigers, and camels he had imported from faraway lands.

Howletts Wild Animal Park provided much inspiration for my fictional Moorland Zoo. In 1958, John Aspinall, a colorful if not notorious figure, started a zoo in his garden shed with a monkey, a tiger, and two bears. That same year he purchased Howletts, a ninety-acre country estate complete with mansion, so he could expand.

Decades later, Howletts is known for innovative animal care, with large enclosures and natural diets, as well as extensive breeding programs and the return of animals to the wild. Most recently, plans are in the works to send thirteen elephants to Kenya. Like Howletts, many modern zoos are focused on conservation and education and have come a long way from the whims of royalty and curiosity-seekers.

Signed,
Elizabeth Penney

ABOUT THE AUTHOR

Elizabeth Penney is the Mary Higgins Clark Award-nominated author of more than three dozen mysteries, women's fiction, and romantic suspense novels.

Raised in Maine, Elizabeth spent her early years in England and France. She now lives in the mountains of New Hampshire, where she enjoys walking in the woods, kayaking on quiet ponds, trying new recipes, and feeding family and friends. Oh, and trying to grow things in the frozen North.

A STROLL THROUGH THE ENGLISH COUNTRYSIDE

The North York Moors

Ask anyone about Yorkshire, and they'll probably mention the moors, a vast stretch of countryside featuring peat bogs, mysterious mists, heather heaths, and old-growth forests. The area has been made famous through books such as *Wuthering Heights* and *All Creatures Great and Small*.

Formed in 1952, North York Moors National Park, a real place near our fictional location of Cobble Hill Farm and Vet Clinic, oversees more than 500 square miles from the coast to inland Yorkshire. Lands inside the park, as well as animal, plant, and insect species, are monitored and protected. The park has a mission to "seek to foster the economic and social well-being of local communities." Leading business sectors in the region include agriculture—for over a thousand years—and tourism.

Millions of people visit the moors every year. One popular activity is exploring the thousand miles of trails and paths by foot or on bicycles or horseback. With so many route options, a visitor can spend time in remote areas or travel from village to village. Wildlife viewing, bird-watching, stargazing, fishing, and kayaking are other options.

The allure, history, and importance of the moors inspired me to include an adventure there for Harriet in this story. I don't know about you, but visiting North York Moors National Park is definitely on my bucket list.

YORKSHIRE YUMMIES

Grandma Helen's Coronation Chicken Salad

Like many recipes, this chicken salad can be adapted to personal taste. What makes it traditionally English is the chutney, which is available in many stores. Major Grey's Chutney is a favorite blend, made by various companies.

Coronation chicken is nice in sandwiches or on lettuce, as a salad.

Makes 4 to 6 servings

Ingredients:

1 pound cooked boneless chicken breast or thighs, diced or shredded
⅓ cup mayonnaise (more if dry)
1 tablespoon curry powder
3 tablespoons mango chutney
1 tablespoon lemon juice
1 large stalk celery, finely diced
3 tablespoons golden raisins
Salt and pepper to taste

Directions:

Put cooked chicken into a bowl and add other ingredients. Mix well, adjust to taste, and serve.

Read on for a sneak peek of another exciting book in the Mysteries of Cobble Hill Farm *series!*

A Will and a Way

BY JOHNNIE ALEXANDER

One last tiny stitch, a snip of the thread, and the gentle application of a bandage brought an end to the lifesaving operation. Dr. Harriet Bailey removed her surgical gloves with a satisfied snap and tossed them into the hazardous-waste bin. A warm glow flooded her as she cradled the unconscious ginger tabby in her arms.

"You're going to be okay, Thomasina," Harriet murmured, smoothing the short fur. "You're going to feel so much better. I only wish you could have three lives, like your namesake."

Harriet smothered the doubt that suddenly flickered to life. While settling Thomasina in a recovery kennel, she mentally reviewed the procedure from beginning to end. The scene played as if she were watching a video, assuring herself that she'd made no mistakes.

She covered the sleeping cat with a light blanket and adjusted the airflow on the built-in oxygen apparatus. "I'll be back to check on you soon," she promised, wanting to believe—as she always did—that the animals entrusted to her care were comforted by her quiet assurances even when the anesthesia hadn't yet worn off.

Instead of leaving, though, she rested her hand against the closed kennel door. She'd felt a profound connection with this cat since its first visit to the clinic. More specifically, from the first time she had picked up the chart and read the ginger's name.

Thomasina.

Immediately, Harriet had been transported to a long-ago visit to Cobble Hill Farm, the same beloved property that now belonged to her. She must have been about nine or ten when her family made the late-summer trip from their Connecticut home to this magical corner of Yorkshire where her grandfather, Harold Bailey, was respected by his neighbors, painted landscapes and animals, and, most important of all, made sick creatures well again.

Though Harriet and her family had made the intercontinental trip several times before and countless times after, a precious memory from that particular visit had been reawakened when the ginger tabby came to the clinic.

"Is everything okay?" Polly Thatcher's distinctive Yorkshire accent brought Harriet back to the present.

"Everything went smoothly." Harriet smiled at Polly as she washed her hands.

The clinic receptionist, who'd quickly become one of Harriet's dearest friends, leaned against the doorframe of the surgery area. Narrow strands of her dark, shoulder-length hair were streaked with a pastel pink, a perfect springtime color that matched the embroidered touches in the knitted cardigan she wore over a cream-colored V-necked top.

Polly glanced down the hallway toward the reception area. Though her shoulders appeared tense, Harriet figured Polly was probably keeping an ear out in case the telephone rang or someone entered the clinic.

A few months ago, Harriet might have teased that Polly wanted to be sure she didn't miss a call from Van Worthington, White Church Bay's detective constable. Van seemed to have won Polly's heart. But when he'd proposed a few months ago, Polly had turned him down. She wasn't ready to make that commitment, and their relationship ended. Neither one seemed happy about the change, and at first the awkwardness between them had been palpable.

Thankfully, the tension eventually lessened, especially with their concerted efforts to revive their friendship. Given the lilt in Polly's voice whenever she mentioned Van, Harriet believed their feelings for each other still ran deep, and she hoped they'd give their relationship a second chance.

"Do you want to call Courtney?" Harriet asked in a singsong voice, though she already suspected Polly's answer. "Or should I?"

Despite the receptionist's spunky personality and talent for making conversation with nearly anyone, Polly would only call Courtney Millington on threat of banishment from the clinic.

"No need," Polly replied. "She's here."

Harriet's stomach knotted as she met Polly's gaze. "Already?" She shut off the sink and dried her hands. "I told her we'd call once the surgery was over. What's she doing here so soon?"

Polly pushed away from the doorframe, scowling. "Your guess is as good as mine. She waltzed in as if she expected me to curtsy or something. It was all I could do to keep her from barging back here."

"Thank you for that." Harriet made sure her clothes were neat then tidied her hair. "Let's go face her together."

"Can't I stay here with Thomasina?" Polly begged. "Just until Courtney leaves. I mean, someone should be here when the cat wakes up, right?"

"Not a chance." Harriet caught Polly's elbow and tugged her toward the door.

When they reached the reception area, Harriet pasted on a warm smile and greeted the woman, who rose from her chair.

Courtney had been a rising star in the fashion world at one time, modeling the hottest new creations on the runways of Paris and Milan. According to Polly, she'd returned home one day about a decade before, with no explanation for her sudden departure from stardom. And she had been a thorn in many locals' sides ever since.

The gossip surrounding Courtney had faded away long ago. Still, no one seemed to know why she'd returned to White Church Bay. Only that she'd brought a haughty, condescending air that didn't go over well with those who remembered the ungainly adolescent who'd been an average student and a snippy part-time waitress at the Happy Cup Tearoom and Bakery.

Now here she was in the Cobble Hill Vet Clinic waiting room. She may have left the modeling world behind, but not the lessons she'd gained in style from her time there. Her impeccably made-up face was perfectly framed by a layered hairstyle with chic highlights and lowlights. Her tailored dress, constructed from a fabric designed with swirls of intermingled pink and lavender, fell from her angular shoulders to below her knees. Translucent purple sleeves accentuated a royal-purple clutch bag, while a filmy scarf hung at her neck. A large amethyst ring adorned her left forefinger, and silver bands encircled all the fingers on her right hand. Her sculpted fingernails sported diamond art.

In a moment of self-consciousness, Harriet tucked a stray hair behind her ear and glanced down at her long-sleeved T-shirt featuring the clinic's logo, and heavy-duty jeans. Insecurity gnawed at her stomach. She'd rarely been bitten by the comparison bug and had no idea why it should raise its ugly head now. Sure, Courtney's fashion sense was glamorous, but Harriet couldn't remember the last time she'd been intimidated by another woman's appearance. Hadn't she outgrown that years ago?

"My cat is fine now, is she not." Somehow Courtney's domineering tone turned the question into a statement. "When can I take her home?"

"The surgery went as planned." Harriet gestured toward the hallway. "She hasn't regained consciousness yet, but we can go see her if you'd like."

"What I'd like is to take her home where she belongs."

At first, Harriet was taken aback by the declaration, but she managed to keep her tone even. "That's not possible. She needs to stay overnight for observation. We discussed that when you dropped her off this morning."

A conversation that had evidently fallen on deaf ears. Courtney had swooped in, plopped Thomasina on the counter, scrawled her signature on the necessary papers, and left without a second glance. Her tires had kicked up the gravel covering the parking area as she reversed her late-model sports car out of its space and sped toward the main road.

At least she'd returned with less ruckus.

"Is it absolutely necessary for her to stay that long?" Condescension dripped from Courtney's tone, which was surprisingly free of a Yorkshire accent, considering she'd been born and raised on the moors. Courtney had come back from her years on the continent with the polished tones of a BBC broadcaster, sprinkled with the occasional French or Italian phrase.

Needing a moment to gather her thoughts, Harriet lowered her gaze and tucked in her lower lip. Advice came to mind from an old boss at the Connecticut clinic where she used to work. *"Iron sharpens iron, and it takes a rock to strike a rock."*

He had meant that an assertive person often responded best to a similarly matched response. From his perspective, such individuals considered anything less as unworthy of respect. That kind of approach wasn't Harriet's way, but she resolved to be firm with Courtney for Thomasina's sake.

"For her to have the best possible outcome, it is vital for her recovery from anesthesia to be supervised by a professional."

If Courtney insisted on taking her pet with her, Harriet couldn't stop her. Surely the woman wouldn't be so heartless as to remove a still-unconscious cat from the clinic.

Harriet met Courtney's glare while keeping her shoulders relaxed. She meant to show Courtney that she was not to be bullied. "If you want her to be well, Thomasina needs to stay here until tomorrow."

Courtney didn't move. She didn't even blink.

Harriet didn't either.

The ring of the telephone interrupted the rising tension. Out of the corner of her eye, Harriet caught sight of Polly snatching up the receiver.

"Cobble Hill Vet Clinic, this is Polly." Her clear, crisp voice sounded louder than usual.

While Polly handled the call, Harriet gestured toward the hall again. "Do you wish to see Thomasina before you go?"

Courtney's vibrant pink lips quirked up at one corner in what appeared to be an amused smirk. "Since she's still sleeping, she won't even know I'm there, will she? Or do you believe animals sense their owner's presence under such circumstances?"

"Cats are amazingly intuitive," Harriet replied. Though many medical professionals believed unconscious humans could sense the presence of their loved ones, she didn't know if the same could be said for animals. However, she'd experienced moments that made her believe they did. "It's possible Thomasina will know."

The dismissive smirk remained as Courtney tilted her head in a condescending gesture. All that was missing was an exaggerated roll of her heavily made-up eyes.

Harriet chose to let the silence continue, broken only by Polly's one-sided phone conversation and the tap of the computer keys. She refused to be drawn into a pointless argument, especially since she sensed that was exactly what Courtney wanted. What did Courtney expect to gain from treating her cat's doctor with such low regard? Or to endanger her cat's life by dismissing sound medical advice?

Polly's phone call ended as the door of the clinic opened. A broad-shouldered man with pale blond hair and a scruffy beard entered the waiting room. Except for his clothes and the fact that he carried an electronic tablet, he might have stepped out of the pages of a history book about Vikings. He removed his tan cap as his eyes, a blue so light as to be almost gray, scanned the room.

"Why, if it isn't Garth Hamblin." Courtney dashed to the man's side faster than a nail to a magnet. A brilliant smile softened the sharp angles of her photogenic features, and the warmth of her greeting removed all traces of her earlier iciness. "Of all the places to run into you. Is our famed vet operating on your pet too?"

Garth furrowed his brow. "I don't have a pet. I stopped by to—"

"My dear Thomasina is in recovery now." Courtney wrapped both her arms around one of Garth's. "Though you may not have heard the news. My grandmother moved into one of those senior care facilities. It broke her heart that she couldn't keep the cat she'd raised from a kitten. And that broke *my* heart. I'm caring for Thomasina now, and she's been such a joy. I'm so glad I can have a pet these days. My schedule made it impossible before, with Milan one day and Paris the next."

"I'm sorry to hear about your grandmother," Garth said, his shoulders tense. "And her cat. I mean, your cat."

"What can I do for you, Garth?" Harriet asked in an attempt to rescue him.

He extricated himself from Courtney's grip and shifted his attention to Harriet. "I stopped in for a quick chat." He glanced toward Courtney as if keeping a wary eye on a dangerous predator. "Maybe I should make an appointment."

"This is fine," Harriet said, grateful for the interruption and determined to use it to her advantage. If he left now, she'd be forced to get back on Courtney's carousel conversation. On the other hand, Harriet doubted Courtney planned to leave as long as Garth was in the reception area. Not with the way she was eying the man.

"Why don't you wait for me in exam room one?" Harriet motioned to the first open door in the hallway. "I won't be long."

"Appreciate it." With a curt nod to Courtney, Garth strode toward the exam room without a second glance. The door clicked shut behind him.

Once it did, Harriet again faced Courtney, who stared at the closed door. Her brilliant smile had transformed into a frustrated frown.

"We were in school together, Garth and me," Courtney said, her voice almost dreamy. "I used to think..." She shook herself, as if ridding her mind of unpleasant memories. Or perhaps unrealized hopes.

Harriet glanced at Polly, who shrugged. Apparently, she was similarly puzzled by Courtney's mercurial behavior.

Regardless, Harriet had to maintain her stance on behalf of her patient. "Thomasina needs to—"

"Stay here overnight. I know." Courtney topped off her words with a dramatic flourish as she glared at Harriet. "Which means I have to rearrange my entire weekend so I can pick up that cat whenever *you* decide it's convenient."

This wasn't the first time in her career Harriet had heard such complaints. Not every pet owner was a devoted one. But Courtney's retort coming so soon after gushing over her grandmother's cat in a futile attempt to impress Garth lit the fuse on Harriet's temper.

Thankfully, that fuse was a long one.

"We're open from eight to noon on Saturdays," she said in her most professional tone. "I'll call you later today with an update."

"Don't bother unless it's an emergency." Courtney retrieved her car fob from her purse and spun on her heel to leave.

"Courtney, wait!" The wheels of Polly's chair squeaked as she rolled away from her desk and stood.

Courtney turned, the familiar smirk back in place. "Don't worry about the bill. I'll pay it tomorrow when I return for my cat."

"It's not that," Polly replied, her tone bordering on indignation. "I wanted to offer to care for Thomasina for you this weekend. So you can keep your plans."

Courtney's eyes narrowed. "You want me to board her for a few more days? How much will that add to my bill?"

"Not a penny." Polly lifted her chin and returned Courtney's stare. "I'll take her home with me tomorrow, and you can pick her up here on Monday. Anytime between eight and four."

Courtney appraised Polly with open suspicion. "Why would you do that?"

"My parents are going out of town, and Thomasina and I will be good company for each other. And that way you don't have to worry about her care or rearranging your plans. It seems mutually beneficial to me."

Courtney hesitated. Harriet could almost see her wheels turning, as if she still suspected some kind of ulterior motive. Such a sad way to go through life—always being on one's guard, fearful and suspicious of others. Though Garth appeared to be the exception. She'd thrown herself at him, even though he obviously didn't reciprocate her feelings.

Harriet could understand why he didn't, but that was sad too. The steadfast love of a good man might soften Courtney's bristling nature, but that man was unlikely to be Garth Hamblin.

Not that he wasn't a good man, but his heart belonged to the animals he tended at the Yorkshire Coast Wildlife Centre, a nonprofit animal rehabilitation facility he'd founded. Harriet doubted he'd be interested in a woman who clearly considered her grandmother's elderly cat to be a burden, in spite of her attempts to lie about it to him.

"I'll take you up on that offer," Courtney said to Polly. Somehow her acceptance sounded as if she were doing Polly a favor instead of the other way around. Without another word, she exited the clinic. A few moments later, her tires kicked up the gravel in the parking lot once more as she sped away.

"I should say something to her about that," Harriet said. "Someone could get hurt."

Polly snorted. "She wouldn't listen, and she wouldn't care."

Probably not. But if something horrible did happen, at least Harriet would know she'd tried to warn Courtney.

The exam room door opened, and Garth peered around the frame. "Is she gone?"

Harriet couldn't help but laugh at his exaggerated expression of fear.

"Until Monday," she said. "Thanks to Polly volunteering to take care of Thomasina over the weekend."

"I heard," Garth said as he strode toward the reception area. "Courtney doesn't seem as fond of the cat as she wanted me to think. Not that I'm surprised. Her mother couldn't abide having a four-legged creature in the house."

Harriet chuckled. "Good thing for me not everyone feels that way, or I'd have to close my doors."

"Anyone with livestock still needs a vet, even if it's only during lambing season." Polly grinned at Garth. "And so does anyone wanting to save a kestrel that got itself attacked by a peregrine. I'll never forget that day."

"I won't either," Harriet agreed. Garth had once rushed into the clinic with the kestrel wrapped in his flannel shirt. The bird of prey would never fly again because of the damage from a larger falcon's talons. But it had found a good home at a small sanctuary near Liverpool with a retired master falconer.

That wasn't the first time Harriet had met Garth. She'd been introduced to him by Martha Banks, who ran a nearby hobby farm and rehabilitated injured wildlife. Garth counted on Martha's help when his center reached capacity, while Martha turned to Garth when an animal needed more care than she could provide.

"I'm guessing today's visit isn't an emergency," Harriet continued.

"Not exactly." He flashed an apologetic grin toward Polly before facing Harriet. "But it is confidential. I suppose I should have called to arrange a meeting, but I was driving past and swung in on a whim. I'm sorry for interrupting your day."

"There's no need to apologize," Harriet replied, curious to know what was on Garth's mind while also concerned that he wanted to exclude Polly. The receptionist had been with the clinic for years and knew everything that happened inside its walls. Her insights often helped Harriet navigate tricky situations with long-time clients. What could be so secretive that she must be excluded from their conversation? "I can assure you, however, that Polly is a trustworthy confidante."

"I have no doubt of it, but I'm afraid I must insist on speaking to you alone," Garth replied. "If the matter wasn't important, I wouldn't be here. Believe me, I mean no offense to anyone."

Polly returned to her seat, gracing Garth with a kind smile. "None taken. And our next appointment is in forty-five minutes, so you picked a great time to stop in."

"Then we can meet now?" Garth asked Harriet as he tightened his grip on his tablet.

"I suppose so," Harriet agreed. "Polly, will you keep an eye on Thomasina? She should be stirring in twenty minutes or so."

Polly pointed to a small monitor on her desk that was wirelessly connected to a camera pointed at the recovery kennels. "Right now, she's sound asleep. I'll go back there in a few minutes and give her a pat." She grinned. "After all, cats are amazingly intuitive, as you told Courtney."

Harriet responded with a smile of her own. "I'm sure Thomasina will appreciate that. Garth and I will be in the study if you need me."

As she ushered Garth through the door that separated the vet clinic from the main house, Maxwell trotted after them on his wheeled prosthesis. His back legs had been paralyzed years before when he was hit by a car. Officially known as the clinic dog, the little dachshund had stayed hidden behind Polly's desk during Courtney's tempestuous visit.

As soon as they were alone in the room, Garth took a moment to greet Maxwell then closed the door behind them and set his tablet on the desk.

"I'm about to show you something truly incredible. I can hardly believe it myself." His voice quivered with excitement. "But you must first promise me that you won't tell anyone. Not your aunt. Not Will. Not anyone outside of this room."

Harriet lowered herself into Grandad's old chair. First Polly. Now Aunt Jinny and Will Knight—the pastor she'd been dating for the past few months, who was the soul of confidentiality—were on the don't-tell list?

Caution urged her to be wary. Curiosity urged her to say yes.

She had no idea how to answer him.

A NOTE FROM THE EDITORS

We hope you enjoyed another exciting volume in the Mysteries of Cobble Hill Farm series, published by Guideposts. For over seventy-five years, Guideposts, a nonprofit organization, has been driven by a vision of a world filled with hope. We aspire to be the voice of a trusted friend, a friend who makes you feel more hopeful and connected.

By making a purchase from Guideposts, you join our community in touching millions of lives, inspiring them to believe that all things are possible through faith, hope, and prayer. Your continued support allows us to provide uplifting resources to those in need. Whether through our communities, websites, apps, or publications, we inspire our audiences, bring them together, and comfort, uplift, entertain, and guide them. Visit us at guideposts.org to learn more.

We would love to hear from you. Write us at Guideposts, P.O. Box 5815, Harlan, Iowa 51593 or call us at (800) 932-2145. Did you love *Snake in the Grass*? Leave a review for this product on guideposts.org/shop. Your feedback helps others in our community find relevant products.

Find inspiration, find faith, find Guideposts.

Shop our best sellers and favorites at
guideposts.org/shop

Or scan the QR code to go directly to our Shop

Love Mysteries of Cobble Hill Farm? Check out some other Guideposts mystery series! Visit https://www.shopguideposts.org/fiction-books/mystery-fiction.html for more information.

SECRETS FROM GRANDMA'S ATTIC

Life is recorded not only in decades or years, but in events and memories that form the fabric of our being. Follow Tracy Doyle, Amy Allen, and Robin Davisson, the granddaughters of the recently deceased centenarian, Pearl Allen, as they explore the treasures found in the attic of Grandma Pearl's Victorian home, nestled near the banks of the Mississippi in Canton, Missouri. Not only do Pearl's descendants uncover a long-buried mystery at every attic exploration, they also discover their grandmother's legacy of deep, abiding faith, which has shaped and guided their family through the years. These uncovered Secrets from Grandma's Attic reveal stories of faith, redemption, and second chances that capture your heart long after you turn the last page.

History Lost and Found
The Art of Deception
Testament to a Patriot
Buttoned Up

MYSTERIES OF COBBLE HILL FARM

Pearl of Great Price
Hidden Riches
Movers and Shakers
The Eye of the Cat
Refined by Fire
The Prince and the Popper
Something Shady
Duel Threat
A Royal Tea
The Heart of a Hero
Fractured Beauty
A Shadowy Past
In Its Time
Nothing Gold Can Stay
The Cameo Clue
Veiled Intentions
Turn Back the Dial
A Marathon of Kindness
A Thief in the Night
Coming Home

SAVANNAH SECRETS

Welcome to Savannah, Georgia, a picture-perfect Southern city known for its manicured parks, moss-covered oaks, and antebellum architecture. Walk down one of the cobblestone streets, and you'll come upon Magnolia Investigations. It is here where two friends have joined forces to unravel some of Savannah's deepest secrets. Tag along as clues are exposed, red herrings discarded, and thrilling surprises revealed. Find inspiration in the special bond between Meredith Bellefontaine and Julia Foley. Cheer the friends on as they listen to their hearts and rely on their faith to solve each new case that comes their way.

The Hidden Gate
A Fallen Petal
Double Trouble
Whispering Bells
Where Time Stood Still
The Weight of Years
Willful Transgressions
Season's Meetings
Southern Fried Secrets
The Greatest of These
Patterns of Deception

MYSTERIES OF COBBLE HILL FARM

The Waving Girl
Beneath a Dragon Moon
Garden Variety Crimes
Meant for Good
A Bone to Pick
Honeybees & Legacies
True Grits
Sapphire Secret
Jingle Bell Heist
Buried Secrets
A Puzzle of Pearls
Facing the Facts
Resurrecting Trouble
Forever and a Day

MYSTERIES OF MARTHA'S VINEYARD

Priscilla Latham Grant has inherited a lighthouse! So with not much more than a strong will and a sore heart, the recent widow says goodbye to her lifelong Kansas home and heads to the quaint and historic island of Martha's Vineyard, Massachusetts. There, she comes face-to-face with adventures, which include her trusty canine friend, Jake, three delightful cousins she didn't know she had, and Gerald O'Bannon, a handsome Coast Guard captain—plus head-scratching mysteries that crop up with surprising regularity.

A Light in the Darkness
Like a Fish Out of Water
Adrift
Maiden of the Mist
Making Waves
Don't Rock the Boat
A Port in the Storm
Thicker Than Water
Swept Away
Bridge Over Troubled Waters
Smoke on the Water
Shifting Sands
Shark Bait

MYSTERIES OF COBBLE HILL FARM

Seascape in Shadows
Storm Tide
Water Flows Uphill
Catch of the Day
Beyond the Sea
Wider Than an Ocean
Sheeps Passing in the Night
Sail Away Home
Waves of Doubt
Lifeline
Flotsam & Jetsam
Just Over the Horizon

Find more inspiring stories in these best-loved Guideposts fiction series!

Mysteries of Lancaster County
Follow the Classen sisters as they unravel clues and uncover hidden secrets in Mysteries of Lancaster County. As you get to know these women and their friends, you'll see how God brings each of them together for a fresh start in life.

Secrets of Wayfarers Inn
Retired schoolteachers find themselves owners of an old warehouse-turned-inn that is filled with hidden passages, buried secrets, and stunning surprises that will set them on a course to puzzling mysteries from the Underground Railroad.

Tearoom Mysteries Series
Mix one stately Victorian home, a charming lakeside town in Maine, and two adventurous cousins with a passion for tea and hospitality. Add a large scoop of intriguing mystery, and sprinkle generously with faith, family, and friends, and you have the recipe for *Tearoom Mysteries*.

Ordinary Women of the Bible
Richly imagined stories—based on facts from the Bible—have all the plot twists and suspense of a great mystery, while bringing you fascinating insights on what it was like to be a woman living in the ancient world.

To learn more about these books, visit Guideposts.org/Shop